WINSTON
CHURCHILL

Man of the Century

WINSTON CHURCHILL

Man of the Century

BY ROBERT N. WEBB

Franklin Watts, Inc.
575 Lexington Avenue
New York, N.Y. 10022

To my good friend John Sterling Hubbell,
who also has a questing mind.

Cover photograph courtesy
United Press International

THIRD PRINTING
SBN 531-00858-4

CONTENTS

PROLOGUE

The Director of Admissions at one of New England's top private preparatory schools was becoming more and more dissatisfied. There must be a better method by which to select new boys from the hundreds of applications received each year.

Had the standards for admission become too straitlaced? Were candidates to be chosen only from the group of applicants with the highest marks and the busiest records in extra-curricular activities? Was the school losing potential leaders because they did not look good on paper? The director decided to test his admissions committee.

He sent to the committee a report on one Spencer Thompson. The boy was supposedly applying for admission to the school for the third form—freshman year. The boy's name was pure fiction. But his record was pure fact—seventy-five-year-old fact.

The report showed Thompson's grades to be: English, 95; history, 85; mathematics, 50; Latin, 30. He ranked twelfth in a class of fourteen.

Included in the report were the remarks of Thompson's Latin teacher: "I have found this boy most difficult to teach . . . He seems to have little or no understanding of the subject except in a most mechanical way. At times he seems almost perverse in his inability to learn. I suspect that he had received help from other boys in his prepared work."

The headmaster of Thompson's present school also had something to say: "Spencer is rather delicate owing to a severe pulmonary illness two years ago, but he seems to have recovered satisfactorily. He is too small to be effective in contact sports, but he greatly enjoys riding and swimming. The boy is certainly no scholar and he has repeated his form twice. He does well in English, however, and possesses an excellent memory. In fact, he won the School prize for reciting poetry last year. He has also, I regret to say, a stubborn streak, and is sometimes rebellious in minor matters, although he usually conforms. He is at once backward and precocious, reading books beyond his years, and yet ranking at the bottom of his form . . . He has, I believe, a native shrewdness and is a manly little fellow, high-spirited and well-liked, who unfortunately has not made the most of his opportunities here. I can recommend him to you on the grounds of general ability."

The admissions committee carefully studied the report on applicant Spencer Thompson. They turned him down.

The facts in the report were accurate. They had been extracted from the records of a young boy who had attended Harrow, the great and historic British preparatory school.

Only the boy's name had been changed. Spencer Thompson was a pseudonym for Winston Spencer Churchill.

1

◆◆◆◆◆◆◆◆◆◆◆◆◆◆◆◆◆◆◆◆◆

THE GREAT MAN

World leader, statesman, soldier, orator, writer, and painter—Sir Winston Churchill was all of these things. And in each field he proved his greatness.

In this age of the specialist, Churchill has been called, and rightly so, a "Renaissance man." Such a man is highly skilled in many fields—politics, art, science, philosophy. Leonardo da Vinci is another example.

Winston Churchill was twice Prime Minister of Great Britain, from 1940 to 1945, and again from 1951 to 1955. When he was first summoned to that post, the highest position in Great Britain's Government, the country was at war with Hitler's Nazi Germany. German armies were crushing all opposition, and England's very existence was at stake.

Winston Churchill was sixty-five when he first led his nation, an age at which most men think seriously of retirement. "I thought I knew a good deal about it all," he said on assuming the post of Prime Minister, "and I was sure I should not fail."

Nearly two centuries before, when England was in

another battle for survival, William Pitt the Elder, 1st Earl of Chatham and a brilliant statesman, put it more bluntly: "I know I can save this country and that no one else can."

Winston Churchill, who said that England's crisis made him feel twenty-five years younger, felt precisely the same as did Pitt. And, like Pitt, he saved England.

The career of no other man so dominated the first two-thirds of the twentieth century as did the career of Sir Winston Churchill. And this is true despite the fact that the first half of the century was nearly over when he came into his full glory.

In the sixty years that Churchill devoted to the service of his country, he held many other high positions in the Government. He was elected six times to the House of Parliament. He was appointed First Lord of the Admiralty on two occasions. He was Colonial Secretary, Chancellor of the Exchequer—a position second only to that of Prime Minister—Home Secretary, Minister of Munitions, and Minister of War.

Few men have been as highly honored as Sir Winston. Orders, decorations, and medals were bestowed upon him by his own country and by nations all over the world. He received England's highest honor, Knight Companion of the Most Noble Order of the Garter. France awarded him the Croix de guerre with palm and the Medaille Militaire. He was given the United States Distinguished Service Medal and was made an honorary citizen of the United States of America.

In 1953, Churchill received the Nobel Prize for literature. When the Swedish Academy announced the award, it said that Sir Winston Churchill had "mobilized" the English language. This he did, indeed. His spirited oratory, his incisive phrasing, and his magnificent delivery inspired the British people to heights of greatness in their darkest hours.

When he was named Prime Minister in 1940, Churchill told the House of Commons: "I have nothing to offer but blood, toil, tears, and sweat."

He spoke in singing phrases that will be long remembered. Germany's armies were sweeping ruthlessly toward the capture of Paris when, on June 4, 1940, Churchill lifted the spirits of Great Britain and of the free world with the words: "We shall not flag or fail . . . We shall defend our island, whatever the cost may be, we shall fight on the beaches, we shall fight on the landing grounds, we shall fight in the fields and in the streets, we shall fight in the hills; we shall never surrender. . . ."

The battle for France was over. Hitler had performed his hysterical jig in front of the same railroad car that had witnessed the German surrender in World War I. The battle for Britain was about to begin. In another speech to the House of Commons, broadcast worldwide, the Prime Minister, his voice never more resolute, stated: "Upon this battle depends the survival of Christian civilization. Upon it depends our own British life, and the long continuity of our institutions and our Empire. The whole fury and might of the enemy must very soon be turned on us. Hitler knows that he will have to break us in this island or lose the war. If we can stand up to him, all Europe may be free, and the life of the world may move forward into broad, sunlit uplands. But if we fail, then

the whole world, including the United States, including all that we have known and cared for, will sink into
an abyss of a new dark age made more sinister, and more
protracted, by the lights of perverted science. Let us,
therefore, brace ourselves to our duties and so bear ourselves that, if the British Empire and its Commonwealth
last for a thousand years, men will still say, 'This was their
finest hour.' "

The fury and the might of the enemy was quickly
turned on England. Hitler's Luftwaffe (the air force)
began pouring bombs on the capital city of London and
on Britain's industrial centers. The British Royal Air
Force, much smaller than Germany's, defended the
British Isles with a daring disregard for danger that
thrilled the world. Churchill said of the British airmen:
"Never in the field of human conflict was so much owed
by so many to so few."

Churchill had that great quality of leadership that en-
abled him to find stirring and appropriate words for any
and all occasions. Speaking to a group of coal miners he
said: "Some day, when children ask 'What did you do to
win this inheritance for us, and to make our name so
respected among men?' one will say: 'I was a fighter
pilot'; another will say: 'I was in the Submarine Service';
another: "I marched with the Eighth Army'; a fourth will
say: 'None of you could have lived without the convoys
and the merchant seamen'; and you in your turn will say,
with equal pride and equal right: 'We cut the coal.' "

Churchill's short, stocky figure was a familiar sight in
all parts of England during every phase of the war. He
would turn up in an air raid shelter at the height of a

bombing attack, wearing his siren suit—a belted coverall. He reviewed troops, visited submarine launchings, boarded naval vessels. A long cigar jutting from his mouth, his right hand raised, the first two fingers spread in his famous "V for Victory" symbol, he thrilled and cheered the English people wherever he went, sharing with them the dangers and vicissitudes of war.

In the American Heritage book *Churchill: The Life Triumphant*, former President Dwight D. Eisenhower gave his personal view of Churchill. He wrote: "Half American by ancestry and citizen of all the free world by the leadership he gave it, Winston Churchill was the authentic Englishman all his days.

"Neither England nor the world shall look upon his like again."

2

◆◆◆◆◆◆◆◆◆◆◆◆◆◆◆◆◆◆◆◆◆◆◆

THE BOY WINSTON

Winston Leonard Spencer Churchill was born November 30, 1874, at Blenheim Palace, Oxfordshire, the ancestral estate of the dukes of Marlborough. His father was Lord Randolph Henry Spencer Churchill, third son of the 7th Duke of Marlborough. His mother was an American, Jennie Jerome of New York.

The title of Duke of Marlborough was first held by John Churchill (1650–1722), English soldier and statesman. For his military services to the queen, he was awarded the title in 1702, and in 1704, Parliament further honored him by allowing the queen to build Blenheim Palace for him at royal expense. The palace was named for the Duke's greatest military victory.

Winston Churchill was born two months prematurely. But he thrived, and at the age of two was a completely healthy, normal baby, waddling around on his short, stubby legs, and beginning to get into harmless mischief.

Lord and Lady Randolph and their son moved to Dublin, Ireland, when Winston was two. The 7th Duke of Marlborough, Winston's grandfather, had been appointed

Viceroy of Ireland by Prime Minister Benjamin Disraeli. Lord Randolph was to serve as the Duke's secretary.

Winston's parents were an attractive, much sought-after couple in Dublin. Lady Randolph was twenty-two; Lord Randolph, twenty-seven. In the endless swirl of political activities and gay parties, the couple had little time for their infant son. But young Winston was well cared for by his nanny, Mrs. Elizabeth Everest. She was nicknamed "Woom" or "Woomany" by Winston and his brother Jack Strange Spencer Churchill, who was born in 1880, while the Churchills were in Ireland.

It was Woom who heard Winston's prayers as she put him to bed each night. She remained his chief confidante until her death when Winston was twenty. It was to Woom that Winston came with his childish problems and the woes that beset him during his growth to manhood. Winston was never close to his father, an austere man more concerned with politics than with the upbringing of his son. But the young man did become exceptionally close to his mother after Woom's death.

Woom tried to teach her young charge the ABC's and simple arithmetic. But even at the tender age of five, the redheaded, freckle-faced, snub-nosed boy showed an intense dislike for school. He brushed aside all study in favor of playing war with his toy soldiers, or riding his donkey.

In 1881, the Churchill family moved back to England, settling in London. Lord Randolph devoted all his time to politics and was soon on the path to becoming a brilliant figure in Great Britain's political life. Lady Randolph was swept up in an endless round of parties in the highest echelons of London's social life. Again, the boy was neglected, for his parents showed little interest in him. Woom remained his closest companion.

Winston was seven when his father decided that it was time for the child to be sent away to school. Lord Randolph selected St. George's at Ascot, a fashionable and expensive school that prepared boys for Eton and Harrow. In Sir Winston's later writings, he always called St. George's "St. James'," perhaps because he had said many harsh things about his life at school and wished to conceal its true identity.

School days for Winston were the most unhappy part of his life. He was never able to adapt himself to the discipline of education.

Winston was one month short of his eighth birthday when he entered St. George's, and school had already been under way for five weeks. The young boy was taken into the office of the Latin master. Outside, Winston could hear the shouts and laughter of other students. He was told to learn the first declension of the Latin noun *mensa,* and was given half an hour to memorize it.

When the Latin master returned, Winston rattled off the declension perfectly. The master approved. But Winston did not understand a word of what he had just memorized.

"What does it mean, sir?" Winston asked.

"Mensa means a table," the master replied.

Winston was still not satisfied.

"Then why does it also mean '*O table*'?"

"O table—you would use that in addressing a table. You would use it in speaking to a table."

Winston was astounded.

"But I never do," he said.

The Latin master lost no time in pointing out to the boy that if he continued to be impertinent, he would be punished, and severely so.

This was Winston Churchill's introduction to Latin.

Winston grew more and more unhappy during his stay at St. George's. At the end of the summer term of 1884, it was decided to remove him from the school. Why Lord and Lady Randolph took this step is not known. However, the decision was probably influenced by Woom, who saw unhappiness deepening in the boy and spoke about it to his mother. There was still little warmth or understanding between Winston and his parents.

Young Winston's next school, located at Brighton on the southern coast, was run by two elderly spinsters, the Misses Thomson. The school was small and unpretentious, and Winston found a kindness and sympathy completely lacking at St. George's.

Winston was permitted to study more or less as he pleased, and he did well in his favorite subjects, history, French, and poetry, which he learned by heart. Swimming and riding were readily available, and when the boy was not studying—which was often—he could be found in the water or on horseback. During his stay at the Misses Thomson's, he contracted a severe case of pneumonia, and for a time it appeared that he would not recover.

While Winston was at school, Lord Randolph had risen rapidly in politics. He was appointed Secretary of State for India in 1885. The following year he was named Chancellor of the Exchequer, the second most powerful position in the British Government.

After two years at Thomson's, Winston was twelve, and it was time for him to move on to another school. Breaking a tradition of six generations in the Churchill family, his parents chose Harrow.

3

◆◆◆◆◆◆◆◆◆◆◆◆◆◆◆◆◆◆◆◆◆◆◆◆◆◆◆◆◆◆◆◆◆◆◆◆◆

AT HARROW AND SANDHURST

Winston's father had gone to Eton, the most famous of all of England's public schools. The term "public school" in Britain means the exact opposite from public schools in America. English public schools are expensive, private, and generally attended by children of titled and wealthy families.

Six generations of Churchills in direct descent from the 3rd Duke of Marlborough went to Eton. The 3rd Duke attended in 1772; Lord Randolph, in 1862. It is strange but true that young Winston did not know that his father had gone to Eton—another evidence of the great void in their relationship.

Winston was quite excited about the prospect of going to Harrow. He had hated St. George's, had endured Misses Thomson's, and apparently felt that any change had to be for the better. His last term at the Brighton school was spent in cramming for his entrance examinations to Harrow. He felt quite confident of success, mentioning in one letter to his mother that he believed he had made great

improvement in Latin. If he had, the improvement failed
to show up when he took the exam.

The young boy was given the Latin questions. He carefully wrote his name at the top of the blank page. Then
he scanned the questions, and found that he was unable
to answer a single one. After two hours, the proctors col-
lected the papers. Winston's remained blank, save for his
name at the top, and some smudges that got on the paper
during the two-hour examination period.

Despite this complete failure, Winston was accepted
into Harrow. Reverend J. E. C. Welldon, the headmaster
must have had many qualms about allowing the boy to
enter the school. He was undoubtedly swayed by the
young man's distinguished father, and no doubt felt that
the son of such a brilliant man could not be a complete
dunce and would prove himself during his stay.

So Winston entered Harrow in April, 1888. He spent
four and one half years there, all of them at the bottom
of his form.

He absolutely refused to learn Latin or Greek, except
the Greek alphabet. English, however, did appeal to him,
and he worked hard at parsing and syntax. Years later
he wrote in *My Early Life:* "Thus I got into my bones the
essential structure of the ordinary British sentence—which
is a noble thing. And when in after years my schoolfel-
lows who had won prizes and distinction for writing
beautiful Latin poetry and pithy Greek epigrams had to
come down again to common English, to earn their living
or make their way, I did not feel myself at any disadvan-
tage."

Throughout his stay at Harrow, Winston refused to

conform, and demonstrated his continued hatred of study. Not surprisingly, he was unpopular with his teachers. His one triumph, however, was winning a prize for reciting poetry. The boy had a truly phenomenal memory. He memorized and recited, without a single error, twelve hundred lines of verse of Thomas Macaulay's *Lays of Ancient Rome.*

Winston also demonstrated his extreme self-confidence. He was once caned (beaten with a cane) by another student. This was a privilege granted to the older boys at Harrow in disciplining the younger ones. After the caning, Winston turned to the boy and said, "I shall be a greater man than you."

His independence was demonstrated when the headmaster called him in for some infraction. "I have grave reason to be displeased with you," the headmaster said.

Winston replied: "And I, sir, have grave reason to be displeased with you."

Winston was no more popular with his fellow students than he was with his instructors. On one occasion, seeing a small boy standing, fully clothed, at the edge of a swimming pool, Winston crept up behind the boy and pushed him into the water. Much to his amazement, Winston found out that the boy was Lee Amery, a sixth former, who was also head of his house. But Winston was quick to apologize. "You're so small," he said, "I took you for a fourth former." Realizing he had only made things worse, he added, "But my father is small, too, and he is a great man."

This hurried apology—and more hurried second explanation—sent Amery into a fit of laughter. He came out of it by warning Winston to be more careful in the future. Years later, Amery and Churchill held posts in many of the same cabinets.

Winston was a loner. He had no friends and apparently wanted none. What he did, he did by himself. One such lonely adventure could have caused him serious injury. On the outskirts of Harrow was an old, abandoned building, naturally called the "haunted house." Legend had it that there was a secret passage from the bottom of an ancient well in the yard to the parish church. Winston decided to investigate. He built a "bomb" by filling a bottle with powder and attaching a homemade fuse. He dropped the bomb, with the fuse lighted, into the well. Moments passed. Nothing happened. Winston leaned over the well, his head sticking down. The bomb exploded with a tremendous bang. His face was blackened, his hair singed, and he was knocked flat on his back. Neighbors heard the noise and rushed to the scene. One kindly lady took Winston back to her house. She washed his face, found that he had no injuries, and sent him on his way.

"I'll probably get the bag for this," Winston told the woman, meaning that he would be tossed out of Harrow. But the school authorities apparently never heard of the incident, and Winston's fears of dismissal were never realized.

It was during a holiday at home, in Winston's fourteenth year, that his future education was decided for him. In the upstairs nursery, he was playing with his toy soldiers—fifteen hundred of them. Suddenly Lord Randolph entered the room, and stood silently as his son put his soldiers through several intricate military maneuvers.

"Would you like to be a soldier?" Lord Randolph asked.

Winston was thrilled at the prospect. He was also delighted because he believed that his father had seen in him a spark of military genius. Not until many years later did Winston learn that Lord Randolph believed his son's chances of ever going to Oxford or Cambridge were nil, and that soldiering was the only career for a boy with as few brains as Winston had demonstrated.

Back at Harrow, Winston switched to a course of study the would prepare him for entrance to the Royal Military College at Sandhurst. This school is comparable to the United States Military Academy at West Point. But the special classes did little or nothing for the young man— studying was still not to his liking, although he did want to go to Sandhurst. Twice he took the entrance examinations, and twice he failed.

Lord Randolph was not only discouraged, he was disgusted. He took Winston out of Harrow and sent him to a "crammer," Captain Walter H. James. Captain James was a specialist in cramming knowledge into a boy's head so that he would be able to pass the entrance exams for Sandhurst.

After weeks of intensive brain stuffing, Winston took the exams for the third time, and he passed—just barely. His grades were so low that he did not qualify to enter a regiment, but could only make the cavalry. Standards for becoming a cavalryman were much lower than those for entering a regiment. The fundamental requirements for boys entering the cavalry were that they had to be of independent means and had to provide their own horses.

Lord Randolph was again disgusted at his son's failure
to qualify for a regiment. He had his heart set on Winston's becoming a member of the 60th Rifles. Now he had
to write to the colonel of the rifle regiment and explain
that his son was not bright enough to qualify.

Shortly after the examination, Winston went home before leaving for Sandhurst. During this brief stay, the boy
held his one and only intimate conversation with his
father. It grew out of an angry tirade that Lord Randolph
hurled at his son. Winston had fired a shot at a rabbit
scampering around the lawn. He fired it right under
Lord Randolph's study window. In the midst of the scold-
ing that followed the father's mood changed. He spoke
to Winston about life in general, about the army, about
the boy's future. He talked in gentle, understanding terms.

"Remember things do not always go right with me,"
said Lord Randolph, according to Churchill's account of
the conversation in his book on Lady Randolph Churchill.
"My every action is misjudged and every word distorted
. . . So, make some allowances."

Young Winston hoped that this talk would draw his
father closer to him. But never again would they hold an
intimate conversation.

Winston was plagued with injury or sickness during
most of his growing years. Just before he was to leave for
Sandhurst, he visited his aunt, Lady Wimborne, at
Bournemouth. Winston, his cousin, and his brother Jack
were playing a game similar to the American boys' game
of cowboys and Indians. Winston was the Indian, and his
brother and cousin were chasing him.

During the chase, Winston found himself trapped in

the middle of a narrow bridge, crossing a deep ravine. Jack was at one end of the bridge, the cousin at the other, and they began closing in. Winston looked down into the ravine, which was filled with fir trees. But he thought he saw his avenue of escape. In a moment he had leaped from the bridge, certain that he could break his fall at the top of a tall fir tree. He did not. He plunged twenty-nine feet straight down to the bottom of the rock-covered ravine.

Winston was unconscious for three days. He had ruptured a kidney, requiring an immediate operation. Medical specialists from all over the country were summoned to save the boy's life. Although they were successful, Winston was bedridden for nearly the entire year of 1893.

During the period of their son's recuperation the Churchill family lived in London in the mansion of Winston's grandmother, the dowager Duchess of Marlborough. Although Winston was greatly disappointed at not being able to enter Sandhurst immediately, he found that in London the whole field of politics opened up to him. It was exciting to be in the midst of affairs of state, where once he had only read about them.

Lord Randolph was now in the twilight of his career, no longer Chancellor of the Exchequer and leader of the House of Commons. He had resigned both positions, retaining only his seat in Parliament. Although he still dreamed of returning to the top, this hope was never realized.

When Winston was again able to walk around, he attended many sessions of Parliament. He heard William E. Gladstone, one of Britain's greatest Prime Ministers, speak in the House of Commons on many occasions. Gladstone was no longer Prime Minister at this time, but he was still a powerful man in British politics.

Young Winston was particularly interested in the debates that raged furiously at almost any session of the House of Commons. He was amazed at the scathing remarks one member hurled at another. Once he heard his father attacked most cuttingly by Sir William Harcourt, another member of the House of Commons. Winston was incensed. He was still boiling with anger when he encountered Sir William in the gallery after the session had ended. Sir William shook Winston's hand, and asked Winston what he had thought of his speech.

All rancor had disappeared once the session was over. Members of the House who had attacked one another viciously now walked out arm in arm. This disappearance of hostility impressed young Winston. He compared these word battles to the jousts of knights of old. When the tournament was over, friendships were resumed. This was true chivalry, Winston decided, and throughout his life, he modeled his own political methods on the examples he had observed in the Victorian Age.

Winston spent the next two years at Sandhurst. These were happy times, for he loved the school. Now he actually enjoyed studying. His subjects were no longer the hated Latin and Greek, but military tactics, fortifications, topography, military law, and demolition of bridges.

He studied the American Civil War, the Russo-Turkish War, and the Franco-German War. His love for horses was still great, and in addition to riding in military maneuvers, Winston rode in point-to-point steeplechases, and began playing polo.

In 1895, two months before Winston was to graduate from Sandhurst and receive the Queen's commission, his father died. The death was a great blow to the young man, even though he and his father had never been close. Lord Randolph did not live to see his son graduate with honors, twentieth in his class of one hundred and thirty.

Winston was to suffer another loss, an even greater one emotionally, that same year. His beloved Woom died six months after his father's death. In *My Early Life,* Churchill wrote: "She was my dearest and most intimate friend during the whole twenty years I had lived." (Mrs. Everest's portrait hung in Sir Winston's study throughout his adult life.)

The deaths of his father and Woom brought Winston and his mother much closer together. This closeness lasted until Lady Randolph's death in 1921.

4

◆◆◆◆◆◆◆◆◆◆◆◆◆◆◆◆◆◆◆◆◆◆◆◆◆◆

LOOKING FOR A WAR

In March, 1895, two months after his father's death, Winston Leonard Spencer Churchill became Lieutenant Winston Churchill, commissioned in the 4th Queen's Own Hussars. This was a top cavalry regiment, composed of wealthy gentlemen whose lives were spent playing at war and playing games—mostly polo.

Lord Randolph had left no money for his two sons, and his estate was barely sufficient to cover his debts. Lady Randolph, with money of her own, granted Winston an annual allowance of 500 pounds, then about $2,500 a year. In those days that amount was considerable, but Winston's fellow officers were so much more wealthy that Winston considered himself a poor man.

The new lieutenant—now twenty years old—could by no means be called handsome. But he did have a wiry strong body. Blue eyes protruded from his round, pug-nosed face. His pink and white skin blended into his reddish-gold hair. Because of his birth and breeding, Winston found all doors of Britain's powerful society automatically opened to him. He moved gaily into this atmosphere, finding himself on a social equality with the most power-ful and distinguished men of England.

But although readily accepted, Winston was not too popular. He was highly opinionated, blunt in his conver-sations, and ever ready to criticize. His defensive aggres-siveness, developed by his long years of school failure, carried over into his new circle. Desperately striving for recognition, he poured out his ideas in an endless stream to all his listeners. It mattered not to Lieutenant Church-ill that his listener might be many years older than he and more distinguished. Winston simply talked down those who tried to dispute his youthful, untrained knowl-edge. It was not long before he was spoken of as rude and too cocky for his own good. This did not faze young Winston.

Lieutenant Churchill soon found his social career a bore. He had not become a soldier to promote himself in London's high society. He was a Hussar, and he wanted to fight. But looking around the world, he found to his dismay that there were no wars. How could a soldier fight if there were no wars to fight in?

There *was* a minor sort of war going on, actually more of a skirmish. It was on a tiny island called Cuba, in the West Indies. Cubans were in revolt against the authority of Spain. Although the rebellion was minor, to Lieu-tenant Churchill it was better than no war at all.

Winston had three months leave due him, and he was determined to see action of some nature. He persuaded a fellow officer, Reginald Barnes, to go with him to Cuba. Next he wrote to an old friend of his father's, Sir Henry Drummond-Wolff, then British Ambassador to Madrid.

Sir Henry got permission from Spanish authorities to allow Churchill and Barnes to go to Cuba. Winston's next step was to persuade the London *Daily Graphic* to hire him as a war correspondent. He would be paid five pounds per dispatch (about twelve dollars today).

Off to Cuba went the two young Hussars. They were shown every courtesy, and every facility was placed at their disposal. The Spanish authorities wanted all of Europe—and the United States—to interpret the two Englishmen's visit to Cuba as unofficial sanction by Great Britain of Spain's right to hold the island. Was not young Churchill the son of the late, powerful Lord Randolph Churchill, once Chancellor of the Exchequer?

Sailing by way of New York, the two eager young officers reached Havana in mid-November, 1895, and received an enthusiastic, cordial welcome. Arrangements had already been made for them to go to Santa Clara. There they were quartered with Marshal Martínez Campos, Commander in Chief of the Spanish army. Three days and one hundred and fifty miles later, Churchill and Barnes reached the small town of Sancti Spíritus, headquarters of General Suarez Valdez. After two days the Spanish army moved out to attack the Cuban rebels in the denseness of the hot, teeming jungle.

For five days the column of three thousand Spanish infantry, augumented by the two British Hussars, slogged their way through the jungle. The enemy, if present, remained silent and hidden. On the morning of November 30, 1895, the weary soldiers halted for breakfast. Suddenly rifle fire shattered the silence. Bullets whined over Lieutenant Churchill's head. It was his baptism by fire, and it came on his twenty-first birthday.

Churchill was under fire once more during his brief stay in Cuba. This time he and three other officers were swimming, when bullets began to pepper the water. They rushed out of the stream and dressed hurriedly as enemy fire whistled all around them.

This was Winston's first "war." A few days later, the two Hussars returned to Havana and embarked for home. Winston had been under fire, an experience that no other member of the 4th Hussars—except Barnes—could boast of. When Churchill reached home, he filed several dispatches to the *Daily Graphic,* and they were well received. These articles launched him on a career that would bring him fame within a few short years.

Soon after returning to England, Churchill learned that the 4th Hussars had received orders to sail for India, where they would stay for a minimum of nine years and a maximum of fourteen. The preparations for the tour of duty took nine months, and Churchill made good use of the time. He reentered the social life of London. He purchased five polo ponies, rode them expertly and furiously, giving no thought to the danger involved, and became a crack player. He also became a close friend of Sir Bindon Blood, a legendary fighter on the Indian battlefront. Winston extracted a promise from Sir Bindon that in the event of any Indian uprising, the old soldier would call on Winston to serve with him.

In September, 1896, the 4th Hussars sailed for India. After entering Bombay harbor, the men boarded small boats to go ashore. Churchill rode in the bow of one boat, and when it reached the stone pier, he grabbed for an iron ring that was imbedded in the cement. At that moment, a swell moved the small boat out from under him. He was left dangling by his right hand and he felt a sharp pain in his shoulder. After a few moments, he managed to grasp another ring with his left hand and pull himself onto the steps. His right arm was useless. He had dislocated his shoulder, an injury that would hamper him for the rest of his life.

The 4th Hussars were stationed at Bangalore in the southern part of India. Life was easy and pleasant. Mornings were spent in not-too-strenuous drills, parades, and minor regimental duties. Afternoons were devoted to sleep—from noon to five o'clock. Then the regiment came to life. Not for war, but for the real reason for the young men's existence—polo.

Despite Lieutenant Churchill's injury, he played the game. His shoulder was tightly strapped and bandaged, and although this handicapped his freedom of motion, he became an outstanding polo player for the 4th Hussars. In inter-regiment matches, the 4th Hussars won the championship from the 19th Hussars. Churchill played a daring, reckless, highly skilled, and determined game.

Since there were no rebellions to quell, the Hussars settled down to a pleasant but routine life. It was a life that young Churchill enjoyed to the fullest, although as weeks wore on, he became restless. Realizing that he was lacking in education (Later he said that his education was similar to Swiss cheese: "smooth on the surface but too many holes in it."), he wrote to his mother in London and asked her for books. In a short time, he had abandoned his long afternoon siesta and was reading four hours a day. The books he read and reread during this period included Darwin's *Origin of the Species,* Plato's *Republic,* Gibbon's *Decline and Fall of the Roman Empire,* and Macaulay's *History of England.* In addition, he memorized almost all of Bartlett's *Familiar Quotations.* Without realizing it, he was building a reservoir of stirring and appropriate thoughts and phrases which he would later use in his many verbal battles in the House of Commons.

Reading only increased Churchill's restlessness. He was suddenly seized with a throbbing ambition, a determination to become an important person, and he never questioned his ability to reach such a goal. The idle talk with his fellow Hussars became more and more boring. He drifted away from officers of his own rank and thrust himself among the higher-ranking generals and field marshals. He was soon telling them how an army should be run, even pointing out that India itself was not being properly managed. As one field marshal recalled this period, "That sort of thing did not contribute to his popularity."—an understatement if ever there was one.

On leave, in England Churchill's restlessness and impatience to "do something" increased. It was now the summer of 1897. He read in a newspaper that severe fighting had broken out on the northwest frontier of India and that Sir Bindon Blood was commanding the British force. Recalling the promise he had extracted from Sir Bindon, Churchill sent a telegram asking to be transferred to Sir Bindon's army.

Sir Bindon replied that there were no vacancies on his staff, but that Churchill would be welcome if he could come as a war correspondent. Churchill immediately left for India. Now he would see real action. He talked the editor of an Indian newspaper, the Allahabad *Pioneer,* into employing him. Next, his persuasive tongue induced the colonel of the 4th Queen's Own Hussars to grant him leave to join Sir Bindon.

Excitement boiling in his veins, the young lieutenant made his way across two thousand miles of India, and joined Sir Bindon's Malakand Field Force. The force was trying to suppress an uprising by the fierce Pathan tribesmen. The battleground was set among high, craggy mountains and small villages of mud shacks and dry plains. Churchill was assigned to a brigade of cavalry and infantry, which was ordered to march through the Mamund Valley. Once in enemy territory, the brigade broke up into small task groups. On the first day, the group that included Churchill was attacked by a frenzied band of Pathans. Churchill saw the adjutant of his regiment wounded, then slashed to death by a Pathan sword. The young lieutenant dismounted and rushed forward, firing his pistol. Suddenly, he was surrounded by the enemy. He turned, shot his way through the Pathans, and took cover behind a huge boulder along with a handful of his fellow soldiers. The battle lasted several hours. When it ended, Lieutenant Churchill and his men carried two wounded officers and six wounded Sikhs (Indian fighters) back to the safety of the main camp.

The Pathan rebellion was put down in the next two weeks, and Churchill's first actual fighting came to an end. In dispatches concerning the operation, Sir Bindon praised "the courage and resolution of Lieut. W.L.S. Churchill, 4th Hussars, the correspondent of the *Pioneer* newspaper, who made himself useful at a critical moment."

The Malakand Field Force activity was a thrilling adventure for Churchill, and he thirsted for more. He soon learned that fighting had broken out in Tirah, another hot spot on the northwest frontier. Churchill pulled every string and used every bit of influence to get himself reassigned to Tirah. In London, his mother got him a job as war correspondent for the London *Daily Telegraph*. It took several weeks before the officials were sufficiently pressured to assign young Churchill to Tirah. By the time he got there, peace had come to the area. A disheartened Lieutenant Churchill had to return to the dull, inactive life at Bangalore.

But Churchill did not rejoin the idle activities of his fellow officers. In fact, he now played very little polo. His dispatches to the *Pioneer* and the *Daily Telegraph* had been well received, so he decided to write a book, and he called it *The Story of the Malakand Field Force.* In it he described the engagements he himself had taken part in, and also vividly described engagements that he did not even witness. With his increasing self-assurance, coupled with the audacity of youth, he was severely critical of how the entire expedition had been handled, of the food served to the troops, and many other details. The book had an excellent critical press and was popular with the public. However, much of it irritated the military, who felt nothing but annoyance at this young "whippersnapper" of a lieutenant. But Churchill had backing for his book. The Prime Minister, Lord Salisbury, thought it an excellent job, and the Prince of Wales wrote the author a letter praising the work.

Churchill was delighted with his success, and even more pleased that the book earned him more money than he received as his officer's pay for two years. So he decided to write a novel. It was called *Savrola,* and it was a bad book. Churchill knew it. In later years he wrote, "I have consistently urged my friends to abstain from reading it." The book earned him 700 pounds (about $1,600).

His literary success, however, turned Churchill's thoughts to a writing career. He considered resigning his commission and becoming a war correspondent. He also had his eye on a seat in Parliament and a career similar to his father's.

5

FIGHTING THE DERVISHES

Winston Churchill was still undecided. He weighed a military career against a political-literary one. There seemed to be little future in the military. The general opinion in 1898 was that major wars were a thing of the past. Churchill felt that he was really cut out for a career as a soldier, but not just a minor officer in minor wars. He envisioned himself as another Wellington, a Napoleon, a Hannibal—a great commander leading great armies.

But there seemed little chance that such opportunities for military greatness would ever come his way, so he turned his thoughts more and more to following in the footsteps of his father. Lord Randolph had been a high-ranking Cabinet minister at the age of thirty-six. His son, now twenty-four, decided to run for Parliament as soon as he could.

Then the military picture changed, much to young Churchill's delight. In the spring of 1898, England learned that Sir Herbert Kitchener, Commander in Chief of the Anglo-Egyptian Army, was about to embark upon a full-scale offensive to free the Sudan (the region of north central Africa) from the vicious rule of the dervishes, a Muslim band.

✓ Churchill's excitement grew. The campaign would be an all-out battle, almost a major war, and he was determined to be a part of it. It was not easy, however. The military establishment had grown openly hostile to young Churchill, a mere lieutenant who had the temerity to criticize army methods. Once again the young man started to pull strings, using all the influence of his friends to get permission from the War Office to be sent to Egypt. He was successful. He received leave from the 4th Hussars and obtained a commission in the 21st Lancers. But it was all to no avail. General Kitchener turned Churchill down cold. He would have no part of this brazen young man.

The refusal, however, did not stop the brazen young man. If anything, it made him more determined than ever to join Kitchener's forces. While devising further steps to achieve his goal, Churchill received a note from Prime Minister Lord Salisbury complimenting him on his book, *The Story of the Malakand Field Force*. In the note, the author was invited to visit the Prime Minister. Churchill lost no time in getting to 10 Downing Street, the Prime Minister's official residence.

At the end of a pleasant half hour's conversation, Lord Salisbury told Churchill that if he could ever do anything for him, Churchill was only to let him know. The young man did so the following day. He wrote to the Prime Minister, asking him to intervene and secure General Kitchener's permission for the lieutenant to join his army.

Lord Salisbury did. General Kitchener did not. The general said a flat "no" to Lord Salisbury.

Lady Randolph now interceded. She had known the general personally, and they were good friends. But Lady Randolph's plea failed. General Kitchener was a man who could say no to anyone—whether a Prime Minister or an old, cherished friend.

The situation looked hopeless. What finally saved Churchill was the rivalry between the War Office and Kitchener. Sir Evelyn Wood, the Adjutant General, had long been unhappy about Kitchener's authority to say who could and who could not become officers in his army. He had, in fact, turned down many officers that Wood had recommended. Sir Evelyn decided to use Churchill as a test case. He wrote to Kitchener, informing the General that while he was indeed Commander in Chief of the Egyptian forces, he did not command the entire British army. The 21st Lancers were an expeditionary force. They would not come under Kitchener's control until they reached Egypt. Therefore, Kitchener had no say in what officers were included in the 21st Lancers.

Churchill received his orders. He was to report immediately to Regimental Headquarters in Cairo. The orders read: "You have been attached as a supernumerary lieutenant to the 21st Lancers for the Sudan Campaign . . . It is understood that you will proceed at your own expenses and that in the event of your being killed or wounded in the impending operations, or for any other reason, no charge of any kind will fall on British Army funds."

Disregarding the ominous words, Churchill rushed to

the offices of the London *Morning Post* and was signed
on as a war correspondent. The money he would earn
from the *Post* would pay his expenses. He would receive
fifteen pounds (about thirty-five dollars) per dispatch.

Six days later, Churchill was in Cairo, the headquarters
for the British army. The date was August 1, 1898.

Two squadrons of the Lancers had already started up
the Nile. Two more were to leave the following morning,
and young Churchill went with them. The regiment took
three weeks for the fourteen-hundred-mile trip to the
heart of Africa. They journeyed by river steamship, rail,
and finally marched in full battle equipment across two
hundred miles of blistering heat and desert sand. The
dervishes were massed, sixty thousand strong, twenty
miles north of their stronghold at Omdurman. General
Kitchener, with his force of twenty thousand, was determined to capture Omdurman. The battle became one of
the most spectacular in British history.

Churchill had his first sight of the enemy only a few
hours after the Lancers made camp. With several other
officers, he rode to an advanced outpost. Through his field
glasses he sighted the enemy. They were arrayed in a
long, deep line, appearing like a low-hanging, black
cloud against the white sands of the desert. The cloud
was moving forward. Churchill wheeled his mount and
rode full-speed back to Kitchener's advancing main force.
He halted at a small hilltop, and saw the British army
advancing with flags flying and standards held high. The
young lieutenant hesitated only for a moment. He was
somewhat apprehensive about the reception he might get
from Kitchener. But Churchill spurred his horse forward.

He rode up to the general, saluted, and made his report. Kitchener asked a few questions, then dismissed the young courier. Much to Churchill's chagrin, Kitchener did not even recognize him.

There was no action that night, but the battle began the next day at dawn. Kitchener's men were outnumbered three to one, and the fight was uneven and over in a short time. However, the dervishes had only a few, mainly outdated, guns, and most of them fought with sword and lances. They were mowed down by British artillery and rifle fire. In an hour, the desert was strewn with the bodies of twenty thousand of the enemy.

Churchill described the battle in *My Early Life*. Sitting astride his horse, he was only four hundred yards away from the fighting. The enemy moved relentlessly forward, shouting fanatically. "We were so close, as we sat spellbound on our horses, that we almost shared their perils. I saw the full blast of Death strike this human wall. Down went their standards by dozens and their men by hundreds. Wide gaps and shapeless heaps appeared in their array. One saw them jumping and tumbling under the shrapnel bursts: but none turned back."

Despite the fanaticism and courage of the dervishes, the battle was soon over, and the enemy was forced to retreat.

The 21st Lancers, who had taken no part in the battle, were now ordered to discover what dervish forces remained between Kitchener's army and Omdurman. Three hundred horsemen rode out, unaware that they were to furnish the most exciting episode of the day's fighting.

Riding forward at an easy canter, the Lancers were suddenly attacked by two thousand of the enemy. The dervishes had been hidden in a shallow ravine, a dried-up watercourse. They rose and quickly surrounded the troop of Lancers. The dervishes opened fire immediately, and the British were forced to charge. The charge lasted only two minutes, but the dervishes were defeated. The Lancers lost twenty men and had fifty wounded.

The charge of the 21st Lancers became a headline story even in London. Oldsters harked back to the Battle of Balaklava and the brave charge of the Light Brigade in the Crimean War. Cavalry charges were a thing of the past, for modern weapons had changed the technique of warfare. Winston Churchill took part in what was the last real charge of a cavalry brigade.

Omdurman was captured by sundown that day.

Three weeks after the battle, Churchill was on his way back to London. He had at last taken part in a major engagement. He now planned to resign his commission and devote himself to writing and politics. On the ship, he decided to write another book, concerning the Egyptian campaign that had just ended. He wrote while en route, all day and half the night. The book, called *The River War,* was published in two volumes. Although the public hailed it, the military did not, for again the young soldier was highly critical of the army. British military men were greatly relieved when Winston Churchill resigned his commission.

Churchill returned to India, said his farewells to the 4th Hussars, took part in a final inter-regimental polo tournament (which his team won), and then sailed back to London. He was completely on his own.

6

◆◆◆◆◆◆◆◆◆◆◆◆◆◆◆◆◆◆◆◆◆

HEADLINE MAKER

Back in London, Winston Churchill entered politics for the first time. He stood (ran) for Parliament in a by-election, a kind of special election. He ran as a Conservative candidate for Oldham, a large, Lancashire working-class constituencey. (In England, a candidate for the House of Commons does not have to live in the constituency, or district, which he represents.)

Parliament is Great Britain's governing body, and is composed of two houses, the House of Lords and the House of Commons, the principal pillar on which the government rests. Like the United States, England tends toward a two-party system—Liberals and Conservatives during Churchill's early Parliament years, and Conservatives and Labour members today. The party in power is the party with the most number of members in Parliament. The head of the party in power becomes the Prime Minister, which roughly corresponds to being President of the United States. The Prime Minister is the actual leader of the country because Britain is a "limited" or "constitutional" monarchy. The king or queen reigns but does not govern. All laws are said to be made by the "queen (or king) in Parliament." They are made in the name of the monarch, but not by the monarch.

Churchill's first speeches were well received, and sizable crowds turned out to hear the son of the distinguished Lord Randolph. But the opposition proved too strong, and Churchill lost his first try at an elective office.

Undismayed, certain that fate had great things in store for him and that the moment would not be long in coming, Churchill turned again to writing. Fate was with him. Six months after his political defeat, British newspapers were running front-page stories about Churchill. He had become a national hero.

The cause of his fame was another war. Out of it came a Churchill who captured Britain's imagination.

The South African, or Boer, War was the background for Winston Churchill's first great triumph. The *Boers*— the Dutch word for farmers—had settled in South Africa one hundred and fifty years before the British began asserting their position in South African politics. These settlers founded two independent republics, the Orange Free State and the South African Republic. Fantastic riches in gold and diamond mines had recently been discovered just outside of Johannesburg, in Boer territory. Britain increased her forces in South Africa to protect the interests of English citizens who had settled in the area some ten years earlier. The Boer president, Paul Kruger, insisted that the British remove their troops from South Africa. Great Britain refused, and the war was on. The year was 1899.

Churchill looked upon the Boer War as an opportunity

to further his career as a war correspondent. He went to the *Morning Post* and was greatly pleased with the contract offered him. He was to receive 250 pounds per month plus all expenses. The pay—then about $1,000 a month—was a figure unheard of for newspapermen in those days.

In October, he sailed aboard the *Dunottar Castle*. His only concern was that the war would end before he got to South Africa. Britain figured it could end the war in three months. It took nearly three years.

Aboard ship Churchill met and formed a close friendship with J. B. Atkins, a young correspondent for the Manchester *Guardian*. The two men had many long talks, with Churchill pouring out his ambitions to his new friend. In his book *Incidents and Reflections,* Atkins gives a brilliant and humorous description of Churchill at that time.

"I had not been many hours on board before I became aware of a most unusual young man," Atkins wrote. "He was slim, slightly reddish-haired, pale, lively, frequently plunging along the deck with neck out-thrust, as Browning fancied Napoleon; sometimes sitting in meditation folding and unfolding his hands, not nervously, but as though he were helping himself to untie mental knots.

"It was obvious that he was in love with words. He would hesitate sometimes before he chose one or would change one for a better. He might, so far, have been just a young writer very conscious of himself and his art. But when the prospects of a career like that of his father, Lord Randolph, excited him, then such a gleam shot from him that he was almost transfigured. I had not before encountered this sort of ambition, unabashed, frankly egotistical, communicating its excitement and extorting sympathy. He stood alone and confident, and his natural power to be himself yielded to no man."

Churchill and Atkins decided to cast their lots together. They would go to Durban, then push on to Ladysmith where they figured the fighting would be the heaviest. But when they reached the town of Estcourt, they learned that Ladysmith had been cut off by the Boers.

Churchill ran into two old friends in Estcourt. One was Lee Amery, the schoolmate at Harrow whom Winston had pushed into the swimming pool. Amery was now a correspondent for the London *Times*. The other was Captain Aylmer Haldane, a friend from Churchill's Indian service.

Captain Haldane had just been put in charge of an armored train. The "armor" was a farce. Ordinary steel rails were attached to the cars, partly covered by steel plate. The railroad was only sixteen miles long. The general in command in Estcourt ordered the train to make its sixteen-mile run as a reconnaissance expedition. Just as it was departing, Captain Haldane spotted Churchill and called to him, asking if he wanted to come along. Churchill gleefully hopped on board. That train ride was to bring Winston Churchill lasting fame.

The train chugged slowly along. After some twelve miles, Boer guns suddenly opened up. Several British soldiers on the train were killed and others were wounded. The engineer drove the train right into a mine placed on the tracks. Rails were blasted apart, but the engine was not seriously damaged. Captain Haldane leaped to the ground with most of his men to hold off the attacking

Boers. He shouted to Churchill, ordering him to see if the engine could still be used.

With the help of some soldiers, Churchill freed the train. Quickly the wounded were loaded into the engine's cab and tender, and the train started back toward Estcourt. The engineer was ordered to move his engine slowly so that the remaining soldiers could walk alongside, shielded from Boer gunfire. But the engineer panicked. He began to speed up, leaving the walking men far behind. Churchill ordered the engineer to stop the train. Then he jumped out and ran back to Captain Haldane. But the engineer did not wait. Captain Haldane, Churchill, and the remaining men dashed back in the direction of the departing train. They never made it.

The group was quickly surrounded by Boers. Churchill found himself staring into the barrel of a Boer gun. He and the rest of the British force surrendered.

Three days later, Churchill, Haldane, and the others were in a prison camp at the State Models Schools in Pretoria. No sooner were they imprisoned than Churchill began plotting to escape.

Some sixty British officers were prisoners in the State Models Schools. The prison itself stood in the middle of a compound, enclosed on two sides by a ten-foot-high corrugated iron fence and on the other two by heavy iron grillwork fences.

While Churchill fretted in prison, fellow correspondents back in Estcourt filed glowing reports of his bravery in helping to free the engine, thereby allowing many wounded to return safely to their base. One correspondent for the *Daily Telegraph* wrote, "Mr. Winston Churchill's bravery and coolness is described as magnificent, and encouraged by him, all worked like heroes to clear the line and enable the engine and tender to get away."

Churchill fumed at the Boer authorities in the prison camp. He insisted that they had no right to hold him since he was a civilian press correspondent. The authorities just laughed. They knew who they held—the son of a British lord. They pointed out to the young man that he had surrendered all rights to noncombatant status because of his participation in the train fight.

Churchill knew they were right. So all his thoughts now turned to escape, and the quicker the better. Captain Haldane was also plotting to "go over the wall," with a Sergeant Brockie who spoke the local Dutch dialect fluently. When Haldane told his plans to Churchill, Winston insisted on joining the pair. But Haldane was afraid that the vociferous Churchill might upset all their plans. Churchill was being closely watched by prison authorities—another reason why Haldane did not want to include him in his escape plan. A third reason was Churchill's physical condition. In order to escape, the three men would have to climb to the top of a seven-foot-high latrine near the corrugated fence. From there they would have to leap about four feet to the fence itself. Would Churchill's weak shoulder permit him to accomplish these two difficult feats? Haldane did not think so. But the persuasive Churchill prevailed. Haldane and Sergeant Brockie finally agreed that Churchill could go with them.

On the day of their attempted escape, the three men, along with other officers, strolled leisurely to the latrine. The other men would walk slowly back, giving the im-

Young Winston, looking remarkably like the grown man he would become. *(Culver Pictures, Inc.)*

This is the way the world remembers Winston
Churchill — giving his famous "V for Victory" sign.
(United Press International)

Churchill and General Charles de Gaulle during lib-
eration parade in Paris, 1944. *(United Press
International)*

Top, Churchill with General Dwight Eisenhower before the D Day offensive in 1944. Bottom, Churchill crosses the Rhine in 1945; Field Marshal Montgomery is at the extreme right. *(United Press International)*

Below, Churchill's tour of duty in India.

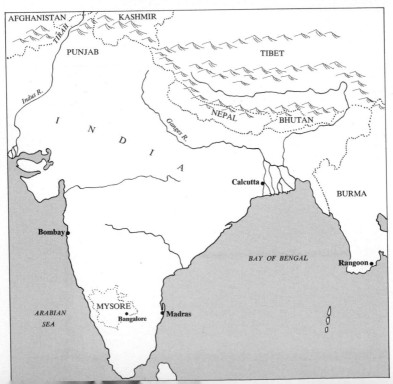

Opposite, Winston Churchill, 76 years old, becomes England's Prime Minister for the second time. *(United Press International)*

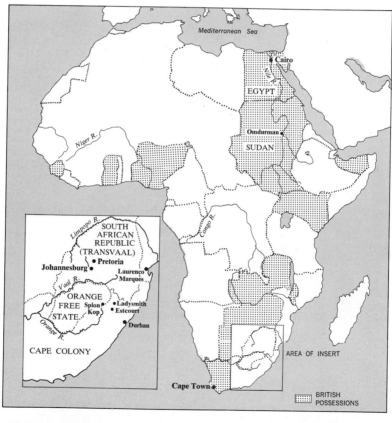

Africa, showing the areas of Churchill's military experiences.

Churchill visits the United States and President Eisenhower in 1959. *(United Press International)*

Winston Churchill relaxes with celebrated English author Somerset Maugham, in France, 1959. *(United States International)*

At 89, Sir Winston remains his old self, flashing his "V for Victory" sign and his ever-present cigar. *(United Press International)*

Amid the ruins of a bombing raid on London in 1941, Winston Churchill symbolizes the resolute determination of Great Britain during World War II. *(United Press International)*

pression that all the officers had returned. Churchill, Haldane, and Brockie would remain in the latrine. Then as darkness and quiet came, they would go over the roof, one by one. The plan did not work. The guard who stood just outside the latrine usually followed the last of the officers back to the main building. This night he did not budge. After a wait of half an hour, the would-be escapers gave up their plan for that night.

The next night Haldane and Brockie, on their own, tried to put their plan in action. Again they failed. But not Churchill. Under cover of darkness, he made his way to the latrine unnoticed. Moments later he was on the roof and over the fence.

For half an hour he hid in nearby shrubs, waiting for Haldane and Brockie. When they did not come, Churchill moved stealthily away from the camp until he reached a railroad line. He followed it for a few miles and came to a goods train on a siding. Quickly he climbed aboard and pulled a tarpaulin over himself. The train moved onto the main line about midnight and started its journey. Churchill had no idea where the train was bound, but as long as it was moving away from the camp, he was satisfied.

Toward dawn, the train slowed, and Churchill leaped off. He headed for a nearby woods and just kept going, not knowing where he was or where he was heading. After many hours, just after nightfall, he saw distant lights. He made his way cautiously toward them and found himself on the outskirts of a mining camp. Desperate, hungry, and near exhaustion, he decided to take the chance that he might knock on a friendly door.

The Churchill luck held. He knocked on the door of the first lighted house he came to, and the door was opened by a tall, gaunt-faced man. Churchill hurriedly explained that he, Churchill, was a Dutch burgher. The man eyed him suspiciously. Too tired to carry on his false front, Churchill identified himself. The tall man's face broke into a smile. He was John Howard, the British manager of the mine. Howard's house was the only one within twenty miles that would give Churchill haven. Any other choice, and he would have been handed back to the Boers.

By a strange coincidence, a Mr. Dewsnap was living with Howard. Dewsnap came from Oldham, the city where Churchill had been defeated when he ran for Parliament six months before. Dewsnap grinned at Churchill and told him that all Oldham would vote for him next time.

For three days Churchill remained hidden at the bottom of a coal mine. Then Howard and Dewsnap secreted him in a goods train heading for Portuguese East Africa. Churchill lay hidden in a small pocket with boxes of wool on all sides and on top of him. Howard provided him with three roast chickens, some wine, and two bottles of tea. For three days the train rolled eastward, and Churchill ate and slept. The train reached Lourenço Marques, and a refreshed but dirty and unshaven young correspondent hopped off. He made his way to the British Embassy, was royally received, and was given food and fresh clothing. Afterward, he quickly turned to the newspapers. He found that all London papers were speculating on his fate. Some reported him not only missing but probably dead. Others said that if captured—and the feeling was that he soon would be—he would be shot. The Boers had posted a twenty-five-pound reward (then about $100) for his capture, dead or alive.

Churchill left Lourenço Marques the same day he arrived. He sailed to Durban where he found a colorful reception. Bands played, flags waved, and the Durbanites cheered Churchill as a hero.

London had the same reaction to Churchill's sensational escape. Banner headlines screamed the story. Things had been going badly for the British in South Africa, and Churchill's escape broke like sunshine over a darkened land. He became a symbol of British courage and determination, and joyful England took him to its heart.

While still in Durban, Churchill learned that about a week after his escape, Captain Haldane and Sergeant Brockie were finally successful in fleeing the prison compound and were again with their regiment.

England's new hero now decided to reenter the service, so he applied to Sir Redvers Buller for a commission. The application posed a difficult problem for Sir Redvers. Despite his popularity, Churchill was still remembered by the military establishment as an upstart. He did get his commission, however, and once again lost no time in annoying the military.

To accept the commission, Churchill had to resign his job as correspondent for the *Morning Post*. Before doing so, he fired off one more scathing dispatch to the newspaper. In it he was severely critical of the way the war was being directed in South Africa. The only way to win, he said, was for Britain to pour more and more troops onto the Dark Continent. "There is plenty of work here for a quarter of a million men," he wrote, "and South Africa is well worth the cost in blood and money. More irregular corps are wanted. Are the gentlemen of England all fox-hunting?"

Such sarcasm did not set well with the gentlemen of England. But the working classes loved it.

Back in the service, Churchill served in the South African Light Horse. He took part in the battle at Spion Kop and in the relief of Ladysmith. Soon he was joined by his brother Jack. On the first day Jack was put out of action with a minor wound. Lady Randolph later arrived in Durban as a member of a hospital unit, and mother and sons were reunited for the first time in many years.

By the summer of 1900, the British had captured Johannesburg and Pretoria. Churchill thought that the war would soon end. The Conservative Government announced that general elections would be held in September. Churchill resigned his commission and hurried back to Oldham to stand again for election to Parliament.

7

MEMBER OF PARLIAMENT

Winston Churchill, always a lover of pomp and ceremony, could not have been more pleased by his reception in Oldham had he arranged it himself. In a way, he had. His South African adventures had made him a national hero, and his reception was truly spectacular.

The town was decorated with flags and bunting. Bands played "See the Conquering Hero Comes." Crowds lined the streets, pressing forward as Churchill passed by, craning necks for a closer look at the twenty-six-year-old hero.

One young lady wore a wide sash embroidered with the words "God Bless Churchill, England's Noblest Hero."

He was "Young Randy" to them all.

Churchill waged his campaign for Parliament on a high, wide, and dashing scale. His books had sold widely and had accumulated sizable royalties. The *Morning Post* owed him ten months' salary. Therefore, he was financially well-off for the moment, the moment being to win the election in Oldham.

Churchill delivered his first campaign speech to a

large crowd that bulged the sides of the assembly hall.
He held his audience spellbound as he told in detail of his
escape in South Africa. When he mentioned Dewsnap's
remark about his vote-getting possibilities, the crowd
roared that Mrs. Dewsnap was in the audience.

The national hero waged his campaign in the blazing
glare of publicity. Almost all the London newspapers sent
reporters to cover his speeches. The *Daily Mail*'s reporter
wrote: "Young Churchill is a genius. The species is not
so broad or so over familiar that one can carelessly classify
a man as such. In this case there is no doubt. He finds it
easier to vault out of a landau than to open the door when
he is getting out to address his electors and win their un-
qualified admiration if he can. He will take a bath thirteen
minutes before dinnertime, will not hesitate to advise or
admonish the Government in a newspaper letter, and
will calmly differ from a bishop on a point of ecclesiastical
law. But, mark you, he is usually diplomatic and consid-
erate in speech and tone; he is boyishly handsome, has a
winning smile, and is electric in brilliance and dash. That
is why people rushed after him in crowds in Oldham, to
see and hear him and to wring his hand."

Winston Churchill won the election. However, despite
the fact that he was a hero, his victory was not overwhelming. Churchill was a Conservative—a Tory—running in a district of working-class Liberals. But he did
win, and that was the the important thing.

Churchill's campaign had been costly, and his funds
had dwindled rapidly. Being a member of Parliament was
an exciting, demanding, rewarding position, but it was
also an expensive one. In those days, Parliament members

received no salaries, and only the wealthy could afford to hold a seat. Churchill launched himself on an extensive speaking tour. For five weeks he toured England, speaking every night for fees running from 100 to 500 pounds. He netted 4,000 pounds (then about 16,000 dollars). From England he went to the United States and Canada. In New York, Mark Twain introduced Churchill's first speech. Advertisements in newspapers and billboards proclaimed Churchill as "the hero of five wars, the author of six books, and the future Prime Minister of Great Britain."

Churchill took back to England 10,000 pounds (about 40,000 dollars) in lecture fees. He started in Parliament with a comfortable "cheque" book.

Winston Churchill was now twenty-six years old. He was on his way to greatness.

The year 1901, when Churchill took his seat in the House of Commons, began with the death of Queen Victoria and the coronation of her eldest son, Edward VII. Victoria had reigned for sixty-four years, and during that time, Great Britain had become the richest, greatest empire in the world. England had changed from an agricultural country to the world's greatest industrial nation. British ships plied the trade routes to the seven seas, protected by the magnificent, unrivaled British navy. Imperialism was at its height, and Great Britain sat at the top.

The Boer War had not yet ended when Churchill took his seat in Parliament, and the fight was still the hottest issue between the Conservatives, in power, and the opposition Liberal party. Churchill listened in silence as speaker after speaker expressed ideas with which he disagreed. It is the custom in the English Parliament, as it is the United

States Senate, that freshman members do not make their first speeches for weeks, sometimes months. Churchill waited four days.

Before making his maiden speech, Churchill did ask the advice of older members of Parliament. Did not his personal knowledge of the Boer War qualify him to break with tradition? Some members thought he should speak up. Others advised sticking to tradition. In the end, Churchill decided for himself.

The speaker who preceded Churchill was David Lloyd George, a Welshman, a member of the Liberal party, and considered a radical. He had risen from England's working class and was one of the most brilliant and eloquent speakers in the House of Commons. He was to become an outstanding Prime Minister of Great Britain in World War I.

Lloyd George was strongly opposed to the Boer War, and in his speech he delivered a scathing attack on the Conservative Government. He attacked Conservative rule, asking, "Does anyone think the Boers will lay down their arms merely to be governed from Downing Street? It is not a war against men, but against women and children." As for the military situation, Lloyd George thundered, "Not a third of the men we sent to South Africa are now in the line of battle. There have been thirty-five thousand casualties: thirty thousand men are in hospitals."

He sat down to the sounds of cheering. Churchill was called upon to follow this eloquent speaker. This was his first address to the House of Commons, and he began hesitantly. He was nervous, and his voice cracked. But he had memorized his speech and had taken days to perfect it. After a few moments, he was in full control. Word spread around the House that this was Lord Randolph's son, and the House suddenly became crowded.

"I do not believe," Churchill said, "that the Boers will attach much importance to the utterances of the honourable Member [Lloyd George]. No people in the world receive so much verbal sympathy and so little political support as the Boers. If I were a Boer fighting in the field —and if I were a Boer I hope I should be fighting in the field—if I were a Boer fighting in the field I would not allow myself to be taken in by any message of sympathy not even if it were signed by a hundred honourable Members."

Churchill continued with a plea that in victory Great Britain be compassionate with the defeated Boers. England should grant the Boers just terms in the peace settlement. He asked that they be given "last of all, but not least of all, what the British Army would most readily accord to a brave and enduring foe . . . all the honors of war."

He concluded his speech with a reference to his father, and thanked the house for its kindness. "It has been extended to me, I know, not on my account, but because of a splendid memory which many honourable Members still preserve."

Winston Churchill's maiden speech was hailed as a triumph. He had carefully chosen a course halfway between the Conservative and Liberal points of view. He pleased the Conservatives by supporting their handling of the war, and he pleased the pro-Boers by praising the enemy.

After his speech, Churchill went to the smoking room where he was introduced to Lloyd George. The meeting was the beginning of a close friendship that would last for twenty years and eventually dominate British politics.

Members of Parliament carefully watched Lord Randolph's son and hazarded many guesses about his future. They wondered if he had inherited his father's temperament. Would he chafe under the restraint of party harness, as Lord Randolph had done, and jeopardize his career? Most members felt that the young man would profit from his father's mistakes, and they awaited Churchill's next speech. He did not keep them waiting long, but delivered a brilliant, cutting attack against the government on the tremendous budget allotted for the peacetime military establishment.

Churchill's attack on the Government was most unexpected. He himself was a Conservative, a member of the party in power. Older members shook their heads and hearkened back to the days of Lord Randolph. They recalled that Churchill's father had resigned as Chancellor of the Exchequer in protest against the War Office's refusal to cut spending. Now, it appeared, Lord Randolph's son was following in his father's footsteps. Winston Churchill, who was to become Britain's great war leader, definitely began his career as an isolationist.

Although never close to his father, Churchill depended upon his father's record for guidance in his early years in Parliament. He pored over his father's speeches, memorizing many of them, and he quoted Lord Randolph widely in addressing the House of Commons.

At this time in his career, close observers always commented on Churchill's boyishness, accentuated by his red hair and pink complexion. The *Daily Mail* correspondent covering the House of Commons wrote: "Sitting in the corner seat from which his father delivered his last speech in the House of Commons, he follows every important speech delivered from the opposition with an alertness, a mental agility, which develops itself in various ways. Occasionally a sort of mischievous, schoolboy grin settles over his chubby face as he listens to some ridiculous argument; now and then he becomes thoughtful and scribbles down a rebutting fact or fresh argument and passes the note to a Minister below who is going to speak next; at other times Mr. Gibson Bowles, sitting by his side, whispers some caustic and amusing comment in his ear, and the long, strong fingers, which clutch each other so frequently in nervous excitement, are held over the lower part of his face so as to conceal the smile or laugh."

All boyishness disappeared when Churchill rose to begin his speech. His words were carefully chosen, his manner of address that of a member many years his elder. In his attack on military spending, Churchill concluded by urging the government to maintain a strong navy and to go to all extremes to avoid a continental war. His plea was eloquent.

"Now, when mighty populations are impelled against each other, each individual, severely embittered and inflamed, when the resources of science and civilization sweep away everything that might mitigate their fury, a European war can only end in the ruin of the vanquished and the scarcely less fatal commercial dislocation and exhaustion of the conquerors. The Secretary of War knows that if we went to war with any great power his three Army corps would scarcely serve as a vanguard. If we are hated they will not make us loved; if we are in danger, they will not make us safe. They are enough to irritate; they are not enough to overawe. Yet, while they cannot make us invulnerable, they may very likely make us venturesome. We shall make a fatal bargain if we allow the moral force which this country has so long exerted to become diminished, or perhaps even destroyed for the sake of this costly trumpery, dangerous military plaything on which the Secretary of State has set his heart."

This address, coming a short four months after his maiden speech, was hailed as another triumph for the young member. The Liberal party was gleeful. The Conservatives were apprehensive. Was this brilliant young party member slipping away from them? Was he becoming too radical? Would he switch over to the opposition? Churchill was to do exactly that.

J. B. Atkins, correspondent for the Manchester *Guardian,* was in the press gallery when Churchill made his stirring speech. Atkins wrote, "He was a lonely but self-possessed figure as he stood there reproducing the sentiments which caused the dramatic resignation of his father. His metaphors were bold and a trifle too ornate here and there, but they were always original and striking. His voice was not really a defect, for it is a distinguishing possession that makes him unlike anyone else to listen to." Atkins was referring to the lisp that Churchill fought against all his life.

8

◆◆◆◆◆◆◆◆◆◆◆◆◆◆◆◆◆◆◆◆◆◆◆◆◆◆◆◆◆◆◆◆◆

CHURCHILL'S FORESIGHT

In the next three years, the breach between Churchill and his Conservative party widened greatly. Jeers and cat-calls from members of his own party often drowned out his speeches in the House of Commons. An unprecedented incident took place during one of his speeches which led to his switch to the Liberal party.

Churchill rose to speak. He had talked only a few minutes when Prime Minister Arthur Balfour rose from his seat. Silence settled over the House. Churchill directed his attention to the figure of the Prime Minister, who was standing alone. Then Balfour started to walk to the exit. Immediately all Conservative members followed him. The party had walked out on one of its own members.

Churchill took his own walk the next day. He walked from the Conservative side of the House to the Liberal side, where he sat next to Lloyd George. This was in 1904, and Churchill, at thirty years old, had been a member of Parliament for three years. He had already lost the support of leaders in his own district of Oldham. They did not ask him to resign but made it clear that he would not be approved for reelection.

In December, 1905, the Conservative Government fell, and the Liberal party took over, headed by Henry Campbell-Bannerman as Prime Minister. His first act was to dissolve the Parliament and call for a general election the following month. Churchill ran as a Liberal candidate from the Northwest Manchester district.

The Liberal party swept the election by an overwhelming majority, and Churchill retained his seat in the House of Commons.

Prime Minister Campbell-Bannerman appointed Churchill as the Undersecretary for the Colonies. Conservatives, friends, and members of his family felt that the young man had betrayed his own class, and they were outspoken about it. Churchill dismissed the criticism with a shrug of his shoulders.

As hard as he worked at his political career, Churchill did not give up his interest in writing. While serving as Undersecretary for the Colonies, he wrote a two-volume biography of his father. It was entitled *Lord Randolph* and is considered one of Churchill's best pieces of writing.

In the next few years, Churchill's star continued to rise on Britain's political scene. In 1908, Prime Minister Campbell-Bannerman died, and Herbert Asquith succeeded him. Lloyd George succeeded Asquith as Chancellor of the Exchequer, and Churchill succeeded Lloyd George as president of the Board of Trade. Churchill, at the age of thirty-four, now held Cabinet status. He reached it two years before the time he had set for himself—the age of thirty-six, when his father had become a Cabinet member.

Despite his rising importance in Britain's political affairs, all did not go smoothly for Churchill. To accept his Cabinet post in those days, British law required that Churchill be reelected to his seat from Northwest Manchester in a by-election. The seat had been traditionally Tory (or Conservative), until Churchill's victory as a Liberal in the party's sweep two years before. The issue was now woman's suffrage. Churchill publicly pledged wholehearted support for the vote for women. But this was not enough for his constituents. One resident in the Manchester district was the celebrated feminist Mrs. Christabel Pankhurst. Her crusade for the vote for women singled Churchill out as the main target. Her aim was unfair, but Mrs. Pankhurst insisted that for Churchill to prove his support of her cause, he must persuade the Prime Minister to openly declare in favor of woman's suffrage. Churchill was in no position to do so.

Churchill was defeated by his Conservative opponent, Joynson-Hicks. The Conservatives were exultant because, at last, Churchill had met his downfall. The *Morning Post,* strongly conservative, hailed Churchill's defeat in stinging words: "At this moment Mr. Joynson-Hicks is the Member from Northwest Manchester, and Mr. Winston Churchill, though a Cabinet Minister, is a political Ishmaelite wandering around as an object of compassion and commiseration. Manchester has washed its hands of him. The juveniles have for days past been singing to a popular air 'Good-bye Winnie, you must leave us,' and 'Winnie' has gone. On the whole, Manchester appears to be taking the sorrowful parting with composure."

The gleeful chortles of the Conservatives and the "I-told-you-so's" of Churchill's friends and relatives were short-lived. On the heels of his defeat came a telegram from the heavily liberal stronghold of Dundee, Scotland. The wire asked Churchill to stand for election.

While campaigning in Dundee, Churchill met and at first sight fell in love with Miss Clementine Hozier. The beautiful, oval-faced young girl was the daughter of the late Colonel H. M. Hozier and Lady Blanche Hozier, and a granddaughter of the Countess of Airlie. The Countess was a devoted and active supporter of the Liberal party.

It was not just Clementine's beauty that attracted Churchill. The young lady had a lively intelligence, was high-spirited, and showed a keen interest in politics. Until he met Clementine, Churchill had shown little interest in women. But now, he put aside politics—briefly—and devoted his full attention to wooing Miss Hozier. He was successful.

St. Margaret's Church in Westminster was the scene of the wedding, and the church was packed. Newspapers sent their top society reporters to cover the event. Anything Winston Churchill did was big news. Wilfred Blunt, who attended the ceremony, wrote in his diary: "The bride was pale, as was the bridegroom. He has gained in appearance since I saw him last, and has a powerful if ugly face. Winston's responses were clearly made in a pleasant voice, Clementine's inaudible." They were married September 12, 1908.

The union of Winston Churchill and Clementine Hozier became one of the happiest marriages of the twentieth century.

Churchill and Lloyd George were now the dominant

figures in British politics, considered by friend and foe alike as the wisest, most dynamic men in England. Even though Churchill was as well known as Lloyd George, Winston was accorded the number two spot, and he himself admitted that the ranking was fair.

In 1910, Churchill left his position as president of the Board of Trade to take the powerful Cabinet post of Home Secretary. He directed the activities of public welfare, immigration, public works, prisons, and the London police and fire departments.

But Churchill had his troubles as Home Secretary. A series of strikes by dockmen and railroad workers became so violent that to maintain order, Churchill was forced to call out troops. Many workers were killed in the disorders, and the Home Secretary was denounced by the unions for his part in the bloodshed.

This Cabinet post would have taken all the energies and abilities of an ordinary man. But Churchill was not an ordinary man. He also found time to study in detail the situation on the continent, paying particular attention to Germany.

The course of Churchill's career was changed by two events in 1911, one leading to the other. The first occurred in July. A German gunboat, the *Panther,* was spotted off the small Atlantic port of Agadir on the coast of North Africa in what appeared to be a direct challenge to further French expansion in the Mediterranean area. England and France had signed a mutual aid pact in 1904; the French agreeing to give England a free hand in her Egyptian activities, the British agreeing to aid France in her desire to add Morocco to her colonial empire.

The Agadir incident kept lights burning around the clock in the chancelleries of Europe, and for three months the continent seemed on the brink of war. The *Panther* stood as a defiant German challenge to the naval power of Great Britain.

Churchill was aware that Germany wished to build a large navy, and he wondered why. He recalled that the Germans had issued a new Fleet Law in 1900. With growing apprehension, he read the preamble of the law: "In order to protect German trade and commerce under existing conditions, only one thing will suffice; namely, Germany must possess a battle fleet of such strength that, even for the most powerful naval adversary, a war would involve such risks as to make that Power's own supremacy doubtful."

Churchill knew that the "power" referred to in the preamble could only be Great Britain. Germany had the greatest army on the continent, and by 1911, she had built up a powerful navy as well. Again Churchill questioned himself. Against whom did Germany intend to use her new naval might? The answer was obvious—Great Britain. As obvious as that answer seems to have been, Churchill was almost alone among the statesmen of Europe to realize it.

Parliament was not in session during the hot August weeks of 1911. But Churchill remained in London, bombarding the War and Foreign offices with questions. He studied every aspect of what he firmly believed to be an upcoming struggle for the rule of Europe.

Fully equipped with facts, firmly convinced that he was right, Churchill now besieged the Cabinet with suggestions as to how England should prepare itself for war. Churchill's ideas met with a rather cool reception by Cabinet members and press alike. In a sketch of Churchill in the *Daily News,* a correspondent wrote: "Hence his horrific picture of the German menace. He believes it all because his mind once seized with an idea works with enormous velocity around it, intensifies it, makes it shadow the whole sky. In the theatre of his mind it is always the hour of fate and the crack of doom."

In one memorandum to the War Office, Churchill enumerated a minutely detailed timetable of war with Germany. He stated unequivocally that Germany would strike first at France. He stressed his belief that England was placing too much faith in the strength of the French army. With prophetic accuracy he affirmed that by the twentieth day of war, the French would be "driven from the line of the Meuse and will be falling back on Paris in the south." By the fortieth day of war, he declared, the German armies would be extended at full strength on all fronts. It would then be time for the Allies to launch a counterstroke in force.

Sir Henry Wilson, a general and a member of Britain's Imperial Chiefs of Staff, referred to the document as "ridiculous and fantastic—a silly memorandum." He was wrong. Germany would invade France, as Churchill predicted, and the Battle of the Marne would be lost by the Germans on the forty-second day of the war.

Churchill's memorandum was written almost three years before the first shot of World War I was fired.

Although the military establishment—remembering Churchill only too well—was disdainful of his suggestions,

Churchill was made a member of the Committee of
Imperial Defense. The committee was composed of the
Prime Minister, the Foreign Secretary, the Chancellor of
the Exchequer, and the War Minister. It was, in effect,
a cabinet within the Cabinet.

The second event which marked the turning point in
Churchill's career was his being named First Lord of the
Admiralty.

9

◆◆◆◆◆◆◆◆◆◆◆◆◆◆◆

WORLD WAR I

Prime Minister Asquith had a difficult decision to make. He had to choose between two outstanding public servants for the all-important position of First Lord of the Admiralty. General Sir Aylmer Haldane, Minister of War, was one candidate; Churchill was the other.

General Haldane, with whom Churchill had served in India and South Africa, was a brilliant soldier. He had also done an outstanding job of transforming Britain's army into a modern fighting force. A Liberal, he was a close friend of Asquith's and was anxious to have the job.

But Asquith finally decided upon Churchill for two reasons—Winston's dynamic personality and ability had made a great impression on Lord Asquith, and the Prime Minister felt that it was essential that the First Lord be a member of Parliament.

The Royal Navy now became Churchill's whole life. He called upon still-untapped resources as he threw himself into his new position. Nearly three years were to pass before World War I was to begin. In that time, Churchill spent eight months aboard the *Enchantress,* an Admiralty yacht, visiting every important ship in the fleet. He examined in complete detail the building of a battleship from the laying of its keel to its launching. He insisted, too, that the British sailor have the finest of equipment and the best food. He knew well the value of high morale.

Once the brash young Parliamentarian who fought against a large military budget, once the isolationist, Churchill now fully reversed his position. This brought about a break between Churchill and Lloyd George, not in their friendship, but in their political and world views. Lloyd George was by no means convinced that war was inevitable. Churchill was.

One of Churchill's first acts as First Lord of the Admiralty was to get in touch with Lord John Fisher, recently retired First Sea Lord. Many regarded the seventy-one-year-old Fisher as Britain's greatest sailor since Lord Nelson. By much cajoling and artfulness over a period of months, Churchill persuaded Lord Fisher (who had retired to Italy) to return to England and join him in putting the fleet into "a state of instant and constant readiness for war in case we are attacked by Germany."

The old First Sea Lord and the young First Lord of the Admiralty worked at a fever pitch. They decided two changes must be made. The firepower of navy guns must be increased by replacing the 13.5-inch gun with the 15-inch gun. Second, they must shift the entire British fleet from coal to oil. These were formidable tasks, especially if, as Churchill believed, war was imminent. A fifteen-inch gun had never been used. In fact, it had not even been designed. The big question was whether ships in the fleet could stand the stress of the additional firepower. To test such a new gun would require at least a year. But time was all-important, and experts assured Churchill that the battleships could stand the strain of the new weapons. Churchill ordered the conversion. If the experts were wrong, Churchill was doomed. The fleet —Britain's most powerful fighting arm—would be useless. But events proved Churchill and the experts to be right.

When Churchill presented his naval estimates for 1913, the enormous costs of these changeovers were included. The British public was staggered; the Cabinet was shocked. Churchill asked for 50 million pounds (close to 200 million dollars), the highest military budget not only in British history, but—up to that time—in the world. The breach between Churchill and Lloyd George widened.

In late June, 1914, an event took place which focused the attention of the world on Austria. A Serbian peasant assassinated Austrian Archduke Francis Ferdinand and his consort. That shot, fired at Sarajevo, gave Germany its long-awaited excuse for war.

Churchill moved quickly. Both he and Lord Fisher had predicted that war would break out in 1914. Churchill ordered a test mobilization of the British navy in the English Channel off Portsmouth. This order assembled not only the main fleet but the men and ships of the Second and Third Reserve Fleets on active service.

The test mobilization took place in the middle of July, 1914. It ended on July 18 as the fleet steamed by the king in full review.

Churchill then electrified the world by flashing a signal

to the commander in chief of the fleet to remain mobilized and stand by for action.

He next made a major move before World War I broke
out in full scale. Secret orders were delivered to the fleet
to move into Scottish waters at Scapa Flow. Churchill did
not want the fleet bottled up in the English Channel in the
event of a surprise attack. During the night, the British
ships passed through the Straits of Dover and took up
their positions.

On August 3, 1914, two weeks later, Germany invaded
Belgium and France.

The German armies were on their relentless move. On
August 1, 1914, Germany declared war on Russia. Lord
Beaverbrook, Canadian-born British financier and pub-
lisher, was dining at Admiralty House the night that
word came that Germany had declared war on Russia.
He describes Churchill's reactions in his book *Politicians
and the War:* "He rang for a servant and asking for a
lounge coat, stripped his dress coat from his back, saying
no further word. He left the room quickly . . . He was
not depressed; he was not elated; he was not surprised.
Certainly he exhibited no fear or uneasiness. Neither did
he show any signs of joy. He went straight out like a
man going to a well-accustomed job. In fact, he had fore-
seen everything that was going to happen so far that his
temperament was in no way upset by the realization of
his forecast. We have suffered at times from Mr. Churchill's bellicosity. But what profit the nation derived at that
crucial moment from the capacity of the First Lord of
the Admiralty for grasping and dealing with the war
situation."

Two days later, Great Britain was officially at war with Germany.

Churchill and the navy he directed were ready. The navy's primary job was to transport the British Expeditionary Force across the English Channel to France. The job was done without the loss of a single man. But the fiery Churchill wanted to strike at the German navy quickly. The British Fleet was on patrol in the North Sea, an open challenge for the German navy to come out and fight, yet the German ships remained in their protective harbor at Heligoland Bight. Churchill, impatient as ever, decided to go in after the Germans, and he ordered a strike. British destroyers and cruisers made a sudden attack off the island of Sylt. They sank one German cruiser, smashed two others into inaction, and badly crippled three more. The British force swung back into the North Sea without loss.

On land, however, things were not going well with the British army. The full force of Germany's troops was hurled at France, and the Allied army was being driven back toward Paris. It was one of the darkest moments of the war. Lord Kitchener, Secretary of State for War and the man who had once so strenuously objected to Churchill's joining his army, now paid him a high tribute. "There is one thing they cannot take away from you: the Fleet was ready."

With the retreat of the Allied forces toward Paris, the Channel ports were being endangered and England was alarmed. To buck up his nation's flagging spirits, Churchill ordered a reprint of his 1911 memorandum, in which he had predicted that the German armies would be fully extended in forty days, thus setting the stage for an Allied counterattack. He sent a copy to Sir John French, Commander of the British Expeditionary Force. General French replied: "What a wonderful forecast you made in 1911. I don't remember the paper, but it has turned out almost as you said."

For eight years Churchill's star had been in the ascendant. Eight weeks after the beginning of World War I the luster of the star was dimming. Prime Minister Asquith was becoming more and more displeased with his First Lord of the Admiralty. Every time the Prime Minister looked for Churchill, the First Lord was in Europe, visiting troops, inspecting bases, exploring the trenches. Important decisions had to be held up until Churchill could be brought back to England. The press and pubilc began to ask why the First Lord did not remain at his desk, where he was so badly needed.

Now two events contributed to Churchill's downfall. The first followed a viciously worded speech against the Germans in which Churchill called them "rats." The British public did not like this language. True, the Germans were the enemy, but they must be respected as a powerful, skilled foe. Only days after the speech, three British ships were torpedoed and sunk while on patrol off the Dutch coast. Churchill had ordered their withdrawal three days before, but the British public did not know it. They felt that Churchill's speech had inflamed the Germans, and the loss of the ships, officers, and men was Germany's reply.

Attacks on Churchill mounted—from the opposition, the press and the public.

The first Battle of the Marne in September, had ended with a decisive victory for the Allies, and it put an end to all German hopes for a quick, decisive finish to the war. German armies now turned westward, concentrating their full efforts on overrunning Belgium and capturing the coastal city of Antwerp, located directly across from the British coast. In Antwerp, King Albert and the remains of the Belgium army were arrayed for a final desperate defense of their city.

Early in October, Lord Kitchener asked Churchill to go to Antwerp, assess the situation and, by his very presence, bring hope to the Belgiums. It was a hopeless task. In Antwerp he became more and more involved with military affairs, and back home, questions were again asked as to why the First Lord of the Admiralty was not in London where, the press said, he belonged.

Antwerp fell on October 10. Churchill had returned to London the day before. Although the decision to prevent the capture of the Belgium city had been made by the British Cabinet and not by Churchill alone, the British press and public made him the scapegoat. He was accused of being personally responsible for the loss of Antwerp. Forgotten was the fact that the Belgium resistance, with Churchill in the thick of it, had diverted German offensives against other channel ports.

By the end of 1914, the war had slowed down. Paris had been saved, and the British navy ruled the seas. But the Germans were firmly entrenched on the continent, and there seemed little likelihood of driving them out.

The British Cabinet met to discuss methods of uprooting the Germans. Turkey had now entered the war as an ally of Germany. Could this be an opportunity for the British? After days and nights of discussion and argument, it was decided to launch an all-out naval offensive on the Gallipoli Peninsula in southern Turkey. The main objective would be Constantinople (Istanbul). Victory would open up a supply route to Russia, and Turkey would be cut off from Germany. Another front would be opened, forcing the Germans to extend their armies even farther, and lessening, to some extent, their forces on the western front.

The Gallipoli plan, officially approved by the Cabinet in January, 1915, caused many misgivings, and principal among the critics was Lord Fisher. Churchill and Fisher had brought the British Fleet to supreme strength, but relations between the two men were crumbling. Lord Fisher did not approve of many Churchillian actions. He felt the younger man was much too impetuous. He also objected to the fact that Churchill had appointed several young men to high command positions in the British navy. Now Fisher felt—and he did not hesitate to say so —that the British navy would spread itself too thin if a massive attack was launched on the Gallipoli Peninsula.

However, the plan was put into operation and a powerful flotilla of the British Fleet, augmented by a squadron of French ships, steamed toward Turkey. The Dardanelles were bombarded, and the fleet moved into the strait leading to the Sea of Marmara and Constantinople. The shore defenses of the Dardanelles were wiped out in a few weeks.

In the midst of this success, Vice Admiral Sackville Carden, commanding the British operations, became seriously ill. He signaled Churchill that he was forced to turn command over to Vice Admiral John de Roebeck, the next in line. Admiral de Roebeck continued the attack and ran into trouble. His fleet entered a mine field and three ships were knocked out of operation. The Admiral called a halt to the offensive and informed Churchill that he thought it advisable to hold off a new offensive until the middle of April.

De Roebeck's decision did not please Churchill. He was alarmed at the idea of losing the momentum gained by the success of the first strikes. A furious argument developed among members of the Cabinet, and Churchill found himself outvoted time and time again. Finally, it was decided that the naval operation should be reinforced by a large force of ground troops.

A month went by, a loss of precious time, before troops could be reassigned and transported to Turkey. During this period, the Turks had greatly increased and strengthened their defenses. When the second British attack came, it turned into disaster. Thousands of British troops were killed, more thousands wounded, and more thousands taken prisoner. The beaches of the Dardanelles were covered with dead and dying British troops. The Gallipoli campaign ended with one of the worst defeats in the history of Great Britain.

During this desperate, fateful campaign, Lord Fisher resigned, and his resignation increased British opposition to the First Lord of the Admiralty. When the story of the Gallipoli defeat was made known, the British public directed its rage to Churchill. As First Lord of the Admiralty, the public held him personally responsible for the thousands of lives lost. Churchill's standing with the public had reached its lowest point in his long career, and the memory of the Dardanelles disaster would remain in British minds until World War II.

One month after the Gallipoli disaster, in May, 1915, Churchill was forced to resign as First Lord of the Admiralty, but he did remain in the Cabinet for six more months. When the War Council was re-formed at the end of that period, Churchill was not asked to become a member. Therefore, he resigned from Prime Minister Asquith's Cabinet.

Winston Churchill was forty years old. It appeared that his career had come to an end.

10

◆◆◆◆◆◆◆◆◆◆◆◆◆◆◆◆◆◆◆◆◆◆◆

VICTORY IN EUROPE

A lesser man might have been humbled by his defeat and removed himself from all participation in the raging conflict. But not Churchill. He was too full of restless energy, too dedicated to his nation's welfare. If he could no longer participate as a war leader, he would become a fighting soldier. And so he did. Three days after he resigned from the Cabinet, he joined the army.

Major Churchill's appearance at the battlefront was not received with any acclaim. Commanding generals were wary of Churchill the soldier. They felt that Churchill, given a free hand, might well try to direct the entire operation of the war. Lower-ranking officers and enlisted men were also suspicious of his intentions. True, he had once been a soldier, but that was years ago. Warfare had changed since the times when Churchill had fought the dervishes and the Boers.

Churchill's reputation, of course, was known to all. Once second only to Lord Kitchener in the direction of the war, what was this politician now doing among fighting men? The answer was not long in coming. Within six months, Churchill had won the admiration of Britain's fighting men wherever he appeared.

Churchill was well received by his loyal friend Sir John French, the British Commander in Chief. Sir John offered Major Churchill the command of a brigade. Such a post would elevate Churchill to the rank of Brigadier General, and he would command some four thousand men. Churchill happily accepted the offer, but told Sir John that he needed a month in the trenches to learn about trench warfare.

Major Churchill was assigned to a Grenadier battalion that was under orders to move into the trenches on the following day. He saw no major action during his month with the Grenadiers, and his initial reception by the officers and the men was cool. But within a few days, he had broken through this attitude, and by his cheerfulness and determination to share the miseries of the men in the trenches like any other soldier, he was soon a popular figure.

In London, the report that Sir John French had offered Churchill command of a brigade caused immediate alarm. Members of the House of Commons protested in long and heated speeches. As a result, an order went out that Churchill was not to be given command of any army unit larger than a battalion. So he became Colonel Churchill and was placed in command of the 6th Royal Scots Fusiliers.

Colonel Churchill's reception by the Scots Fusiliers was no warmer than the one he had first received by the Grenadier Guards. But again, he overcame all resistance within a day of taking over. He did this by delivering to

his officers a lengthy lecture on the louse—the pesky bug
that men in the trenches knew intimately. The lecture
was witty, dramatic, and filled with wisdom about the
life and habits of the louse. Apparently, Churchill had
thoroughly researched his subject, as usual. He declared
war on lice. The officers passed on the knowledge that
they had gained from their new commander, and within
a short time the 6th Royal Scots Fusiliers had completely
deloused itself.

Churchill spent a charmed life in his stay with the
Fusiliers. He insisted on being in the thick of every engagement, and he saw fellow soldiers cut down on either
side of him. Although bullets whizzed around his head,
he was never harmed.

After six months of trench warfare, Churchill asked to
be relieved of his command. He was still a member of
Parliament, and he wished to return to London to speak
on the new naval estimates bill then before the House of
Commons. His request was granted with the stipulation
that he would not again seek to join the army.

Churchill was shaken by his reception from fellow
members of Parliament. Abuse was heaped upon him,
and he was bitterly denounced by the opposition. The press
and public remained as hostile to him as they had been
six months before when he resigned from the Cabinet.

Dreary months followed for Churchill. He was frus-
trated everywhere he turned. His family became his chief
interest and his wife his chief supporter. He renewed a
hobby—painting—that he had picked up in 1915. The
year before he had done some daubing with one of his
children's paint boxes. (The Churchills had one son, Ran-

dolph, and three daughters, Diana, Sarah, and Mary. One daughter died in infancy.) Now he went out and purchased expensive oils, brushes, easels, and canvases. Churchill never did anything by half measures.

Churchill's hopes of getting back into the political arena bounced upward when the Government of Prime Minister Asquith fell in December, 1916. Lloyd Geroge became the new Prime Minister, and Churchill felt sure that his old friend would ask him to take a post in the Cabinet. Although Lloyd George wanted to make the offer, he found strenuous opposition to Churchill on every side, and he had to abandon the idea. Once again, Churchill's spirits flagged.

Six months later—a dark, lonesome, unhappy six months for Churchill—conditions had changed. Lloyd George had gained the backing of everyone in the British Empire. He was at the height of his power, and he felt that he could now invite Churchill into his Cabinet. Against some minor objections, Churchill was appointed to the Ministry of Munitions. He was not back in the War Council but he was out of exile. Churchill remarked that they would not let him make plans, but they would let him make munitions.

Now forty-three, Churchill threw himself into his new job with the same drive and energy that he devoted to every task. In this post he made what might be considered his greatest contribution to the Allied victory over Germany. War production rose sharply. Machine-gun production rose 40 percent, tank production 27 percent; and 40 percent more British planes were soon flying over France.

The increase in war production came at a vital time. The United States entered the war in April, 1917, and soon streams of American soldiers were pouring into France. It required a longer time for the United States to switch from peace- to war-time production than it did to raise the forty-eight divisions which America planned to put into France. Guns and ammunition were needed by the Americans, and Churchill supplied them. He undertook to fulfill an order totaling 100 million pounds (or some 400 million dollars) to supply the Yanks' needs. He did just that, and a high proportion of American soldiers went into the trenches with guns made in Britain.

The United States provided the weary French and British armies with the fresh manpower necessary to bring the war to an end. Eighteen months after the United States entered the war, an armistice was signed on November 11, 1918. World War I was over.

Lloyd George switched Churchill from the Ministry of Munitions to the Ministry of War. This job now was primarily to see to the orderly demobilization of British military men. But with his customary flair for deeper involvement, Churchill used his new position to try to stem the rise of Communist power in Russia.

Russia had collapsed and withdrawn from the war several months before the armistice. Revolution had toppled the Russian czar. A radical group of Bolsheviks assumed power and made a separate peace treaty with Germany before the war ended. White Russians, supporters of the late czar, launched a counterrevolutionary strike.

The Allies maintained a small force in Russia but there was a great demand to bring the troops home. In the

House of Commons and in other speeches, Churchill attacked the Reds and even urged sending arms and supplies to the White Russians. But the world was weary of war, and Churchill had to abandon his crusade.

11

◆◆◆

CHANCELLOR OF THE EXCHEQUER

World War I was over—the end of one era and the beginning of another. It could be called the Era of the Common Man in Britain, beginning as it did with the rise of the Labour party to a position of political power. Churchill and other members of the Establishment, the titled members of Britain's ruling class, found themselves being pushed into the background.

Churchill did perform one more outstanding service to his nation before going into political eclipse. He assumed the role of peacemaker, a little-known side of Winston Churchill.

Peace had come to Western Europe, but the Middle East was ready to explode at any moment, The Arabs, who had fought against the Turks in the war, felt that they had been unjustly treated at the Versailles peace conference where the postwar decisions of land and colonial apportionments were made. France was given a mandate over Syria, and Palestine and Egypt seethed. An uprising in Iraq had to be put down at the cost of many lives. At a cost of 30 million pounds (about 120 million dollars) annually, Britain had to maintain a force of forty thousand troops in Iraq.

To cut these costs and to try to bring about peace in the Middle East, Prime Minister Lloyd George switched Churchill from the Ministry of War to Secretary for the Colonies, and dumped the Middle East problem in his lap.

Churchill approached this problem in his usual, unorthodox manner. His first move was to seek out Lawrence of Arabia, the mysterious and romantic Englishman considered the uncrowned king of Arabia. The two men met in Cairo, and Churchill received from Lawrence full cooperation and support for his plan. Within a month a satisfactory settlement of all problems had been worked out. The proposed settlement was ratified by the British Cabinet, and was acceptable to the disputing rulers of the Middle East. The settlement is still considered one of the most brilliant ever made. It brought peace and harmony to the explosive Middle East for a period of eleven years.

Much time would pass before Winston Churchill was again to assume a post of importance in his nation. In the meantime he suffered defeat after defeat. The year was 1922, and Churchill's old friend Lloyd George was forced to resign as Prime Minister. Unlike Churchill, Lloyd George never held political office again.

Now forty-eight years old, Churchill ran for reelection from Dundee the same year, but was hampered in his campaign by having to undergo an emergency appendectomy. Unable to go to Dundee until the final week before the voting, he arrived in a wheelchair. His condition brought him no sympathy from the Dundee electorate.

On the contrary, he was booed and shouted down by the audiences he attempted to address. The voters of Dundee felt that Churchill had little or no interest in domestic affairs. His concern, if any, for the workingman was pure opportunism. He had for too long involved himself in international affairs to be able to deal with the problems of the common man.

Churchill was soundly defeated. For the first time since 1900, he was without a seat in Parliament. His comment on his defeat has become one of his most frequently quoted remarks: "In the twinkling of an eye, I found myself without an office, without a seat, without a party, and even without an appendix."

Following his defeat, Churchill took his family to France. For the first few months he devoted himself entirely to his painting, and turned out several brilliantly colored landscapes. He even sold four of them at about 70 dollars apiece. He carefully signed them "Charles Morin," so prospective buyers would not buy the landscapes because they had been painted by the famous Winston Churchill.

Churchill's serious work during this period was writing. He completed two volumes of a proposed historical work called *The World Crisis*. His capacity for work was truly astonishing. The first volume came out in April, 1925; the second in October of the same year. Although some critics considered the work more of a personal history of Winston Churchill than a history of the world in crisis, the book was well received and netted him some 20,000 pounds (then 80,000 dollars). With this money, Churchill bought his country estate, Chartwell Manor.

In the fall of 1923, Churchill again ran for a scat in Parliament, and again he was defeated. Twice he had been defeated as a Liberal candidate, and so, in the 1924 general election, he ran as an Independent. The change-over did him no good. He lost again—three defeats in a row.

The Labour party came into power in the general election of 1923, and in January, 1924, Labour took over the reins of government for the first time in British history, with Ramsay MacDonald as Prime Minister and Foreign Secretary.

It was a period of change in British politics. The Liberal party came to an end as a factor in Parliament—Churchill had long since severed his connections. The Labour party was now in power—but for less than two years. The Conservative party won the next election. Churchill stood for a seat from Epping as a "Constitutionalist," and with the backing of sufficient Conservatives, he won.

Stanley Baldwin then became Prime Minister and took a step which shocked the vast majority of his Conservative followers. He appointed Winston Churchill as Chancellor of the Exchequer. Churchill, at the age of fifty, was back in the fold. Once again he was a Tory, a Conservative, a member of the party he had left shortly after his election to Parliament in 1901.

The political exile of the past two years was back in the Cabinet in a position second only to that of Prime Minister. Indeed, it was the position considered to be a stepping-stone to that highest of all British offices.

The appointment was particularly pleasing to Church-ill. The office held great political and sentimental significance for him. His father had once worn the robes of the Chancellor of the Exchequer. Churchill dug those same robes out of mothballs and wore them when he first addressed the House of Commons in his new post.

Churchill was now in charge of the entire economy of the British Empire. As a boy at Harrow he had never been able to pass the simplest test in arithmetic. Now he was confronted with enormous financial problems. In all the high posts that Churchill held in the British government, he was least successful in his position as Chancellor of the Exchequer, and it was from this post that he appeared to go to his political grave.

Britain's economy was extremely shaky during this period. Conditions in the coal mining industry were bad. Mineowners said that unless wages could be lowered or working hours increased, they would have to close the mines. The miners retaliated with a threat to strike. The government intervened, but conditions worsened. The miners walked out, followed by all of Britain's unionized labor force, bringing on a general strike.

Newspapers stopped publishing. Prime Minister Baldwin called upon Churchill, the former newspaperman, to edit a government newspaper called the *British Gazette*. The Chancellor of the Exchequer took on the job. He defied union printers by calling upon trade school students to set the type. The British Automobile Association was drafted to distribute the paper. Churchill did practically all the writing, and his columns further infuriated the working classes. All of his articles were slanted in favor of the government and industry owners.

The general strike continued for ten days. The miners

held out longer, surrendering only after they faced starvation. Churchill became the most hated man in England by Britain's working class. By 1929, his position with the British people had deteriorated even further. All his life he had been either the most popular or the most unpopular man in his country, and now he was at the lowest ebb of his popularity. In the 1929 general election, the Labour party and Ramsay MacDonald were returned to power. Churchill was out of office again, and prime ministers for the next ten years would see to it that he stayed out.

12

◆◆◆◆◆◆◆◆◆◆◆◆◆◆◆◆◆◆◆◆◆◆◆◆

"WINSTON IS BACK!"

During the ten years from 1929 to 1939, Churchill spent his time painting, writing, and traveling. He visited America and traveled extensively in Europe.

He did remain a member of Parliament and spoke on many subjects. He vehemently opposed the Indian independence movement and was sharp in his criticism of Mahatma Gandhi, the great Indian leader. He also championed a cause which brought him into further disfavor with the British people.

This was a cause which distracted England from its economic and colonial woes and aroused the romantic interests of the entire world. The Prince of Wales ascended the throne of England as Edward VIII, in 1936. A world traveler, the new king was a most popular young man.

In December of that year, Edward shocked the British Empire and attracted world attention by announcing his intention to marry an American divorcée—Mrs. Wallace Warfield Simpson. Britain was stunned. British tradition was being violated. For a king to marry a commoner was unthinkable, and for the commoner to be a divorced woman was absolutely unacceptable to the British people.

Prime Minister Baldwin took a firm, unyielding position. King Edward could either give up Wallace Simpson and keep the throne, or marry her and abdicate.

Churchill rallied to Edward's side. Ever the romantic, Winston hurled himself into the thick of the battle. He spoke in Parliament, urging members to use caution, to take time and study the matter seriously. Parliament had no time for Churchill, and neither did the British people. Churchill persisted, especially after King Edward called him to Buckingham Palace for advice and counsel. The two men were old friends.

On December 10, 1936, King Edward VIII announced his abdication in a worldwide broadcast, saying that he could not carry on without the aid of "the woman I love." England breathed a long sigh of relief. Churchill's siding with Edward only increased his unpopularity with the British people, the press, and Parliament. He retreated to his Chartwell home and turned his full attention to writing a biography of the 1st Duke of Marlborough, his great ancestor John Churchill.

Although Churchill was unwanted by the British Government and public alike, he did not give up his keen interest in the affairs of his country and the world. On a trip to Germany to do research on the Duke of Marlborough, Churchill learned firsthand about the growing strength of the Hitler movement. He was particularly appalled by Hitler's violent outcries against the Jews.

Churchill returned to England a worried man. He felt that the seeds of a second great conflict with Germany were being planted. At this time, however, the entire world was enchanted with discussions of disarmament plans. Churchill vigorously opposed all such ideas. The year was 1932 and England was in the midst of an economic depression. English pacifists were in full cry. Disarmament meant a greatly reduced national budget. Prime Minister Baldwin went along with the pacifists.

Of all the statesmen in Europe, Churchill seemed to stand alone in his recognition of the threat posed by the resurgence of Germany's military spirit. Churchill had just returned from Munich in the summer of 1932 when Germany demanded the right to rearm. In England, this request was looked upon favorably by many, including the influential London *Times*. In a dramatic speech to the House of Commons, Churchill warned his countrymen: "Do not let His Majesty's Government believe that all Germany is looking for is equal status . . . All these bands of sturdy Teutonic youths marching through the streets and roads of Germany, with the light of desire in their eyes to suffer for the Fatherland, are not looking for status. They are looking for weapons, and, when they have the weapons, believe me they will ask for the return of their lost territories and lost colonies . . ."

Neither the Parliament nor the British people paid any heed to the warning. Only two months after Churchill's speech, in January, 1933, Adolf Hitler came to power in Germany.

As Churchill had been prior to World War I, so he was again the prophet unheeded by his countrymen. His prophetic accuracy also led him to foresee that air strength would become a major factor in a second world war. He knew from personal observation that Germany was building up its air arm, and he urged the British Government to do the same. The British Government did not listen.

In 1935, Churchill estimated that Germany's air force would double by 1937. Prime Minister Baldwin answered that there was no cause for alarm, and he challenged the accuracy of Churchill's figures. A few months later, Baldwin admitted his error. Germany had equaled Great Britain's air strength and she was building military planes at a faster rate.

This admission of error on the part of the Prime Minister in no way affected his position with the British people. In the general election of 1935, Baldwin and his party were returned to power by an overwhelming majority.

Churchill now felt certain that Baldwin would make him a member of his Cabinet. He had supplied Baldwin with a tremendous amount of accurate knowledge about Germany and the European situation in general. But Baldwin had his reasons for ignoring Churchill, and they were good ones. Churchill was still in disrepute, and had no following among the British people. Any position that Baldwin might offer Churchill would bring wild cries of protest from the House of Commons and the British public.

Baldwin resigned as Prime Minister in 1937 and was succeeded by Neville Chamberlain. Chamberlain was in complete disagreement with Churchill's views about Hitler and Germany. Thus, there was no chance of Churchill's being returned to a Cabinet position.

Prime Minister Chamberlain's major interest was in preserving peace. He believed that Hitler could be contained by a policy of appeasement, and he did not change his view even after Hitler annexed Austria. Chamberlain continued to maintain his position as Hitler's armies marched into the Sudeten part of Czechoslovakia, rich in iron, copper, zinc, and coal mines—the basic materials needed to build a gigantic war machine.

Chamberlain flew to Munich and reached an agreement with Hitler. The Führer stated that he had no further desire to extend Germany's land holdings. Chamberlain returned to London and announced that by the agreement with Hitler, he had achieved "peace in our time." The Munich agreement was hailed in Great Britain.

In March, 1939, Hitler gobbled up the rest of Czechoslovakia. Too late, Chamberlain realized that Hitler's promise was meaningless. An uneasy peace came to Europe. Hitler was only biding his time, and building up his military machine.

In the summer of 1939, Great Britain received a stunning shock. There had been talk of an alliance between Britain, France, and Russia for the protection of the central and eastern European states. Such a pact would have done much to prevent World War II. Churchill pressed Chamberlain to work hard and quickly to reach such an agreement, but the Prime Minister hesitated. Then, in August, 1939, fateful news shocked the entire world. Joseph Stalin—dictator of Russia—and Adolf Hitler announced a ten-year nonaggression pact. Germany was free to turn her full attention toward western Europe.

On September 1, 1939, the German Wehrmacht (army) was on the move again as German tanks thundered into Poland.

Two days later, Chamberlain announced to an anxious

world that a state of war existed between Great Britain and Germany. On the same day, Chamberlain asked Churchill to assume the duties of First Lord of the Admiralty.

The mighty British Fleet, its battleships stationed all over the world, heard the news by the signal, "Winston is back!"

13

◆◆◆◆◆◆◆◆◆◆◆◆◆◆◆◆◆◆

PRIME MINISTER

For the second time in his career, Winston Churchill was First Lord of the Admiralty. Exactly twenty-five years earlier, Churchill had held this same position, steering the British Fleet through the early months of World War I. This time, his hand was steadier on the helm, and he avoided the mistakes of his earlier stewardship.

There was little action by French and British forces during the first seven months of World War II. The German army overran Poland. Stalin's Russian army attacked the Baltic states, finally overcoming the stiff resistance of the small Finnish troops.

The British and French stood by, waiting with apprehension for Hitler's next move. Although the British army went through extensive training maneuvers, there was no actual fighting. In America, this period was referred to as "the phony war."

During these months, England's industry worked desperately to build up its war machine. It was now recognized that the German air force had twice the number of planes that Britain had.

Across the English Channel, French soldiers lay in wait behind the Maginot Line. This was a series of fortifications on the northeastern border of France. Begun in 1927, it was considered impregnable. The French were confident that when—and if—Germany hurled her armies against this fortified line, the enemy would be smashed to bits.

On the high seas, the British Fleet was already in action under the leadership of the First Lord of the Admiralty. A blockade was set up off the German coast, and German submarines and raiders were constantly harassed and sunk. Convoys were established, and new ships were under construction. The Royal Navy remained Britain's greatest fighting arm and Winston Churchill made sure that it was at full strength, just as he had made sure of it in World War I.

Prime Minister Chamberlain felt that after seven months the war was going well for the Allies. He made this statement to the British public in April, 1940, with Churchill in complete disagreement. Three days after Chamberlain made his speech, the German armies were on the march again. Hitler invaded Norway and Denmark.

Germany crushed these two small countries with ease, and the British public was aroused. Why had Britain and France stood by as Hitler relentlessly mowed down nation after nation? A furious debate about Chamberlain's conduct of the war raged for three days in Parliament. On May 9, the House of Commons voted on the Prime Minister's direction. Chamberlain came out of the vote a winner, but the small margin demonstrated a decided lack of confidence in his leadership. Chamberlain resigned as Prime Minister.

On May 10, 1940, King George VI, who had ascended the throne on the abdication of his elder brother Edward VIII, summoned Winston Churchill. The King asked Churchill to form a new government. It was the most momentous day in Churchill's life. After forty years of service to his nation, he had reached the absolute top— he was the King's First Minister, Prime Minister of Great Britain. Winston Churchill was sixty-five years old.

Age had never meant anything to Churchill. He was strong of body, strong of mind, and determined in purpose. Now he would lead his nation in the most challenging period of its history. He brought immediate hope to all Britain with his first address as Prime Minister in the House of Commons. "I have nothing to offer but blood, toil, tears and sweat . . . Come then, let us go forward together with our united strength. . . ."

Churchill's first weeks as Britain's war leader were most discouraging. Hitler's Wehrmacht, driving toward the Channel ports, captured Holland on May 15, just five days after Churchill became Prime Minister. Driving relentlessly forward, the Nazis captured Belgium ten days later, leaving the British Expeditionary Force in a desperate position. Pressed by the conquering Germans at the Belgium border into the north, cut off from the French forces to the east by the German army moving on Paris, the Englishmen were trapped. The only chance of survival was to retreat to Dunkirk, a small port on the northern coast of France. From there, perhaps they could get back to England across the Channel.

Great Britain was faced with one of the darkest hours in its history, but the evacuation at Dunkirk proved one of the most stirring periods of the war. An Admiralty radio appeal asked Englishmen to aid the trapped British Expeditionary Force with anything that would float. The British responded. Rowboats, fishing boats, small sailing craft, powerboats, yachts—indeed, anything that would float—were pressed into service. Nearly nine hundred boats of every description moved back and forth across the English Channel, ferrying the British soldiers to safety.

The evacuation by this hastily assembled, strange flotilla began on the night of May 26, and continued for nine days. German fighting planes raked the makeshift flotilla with searing machine-gun fire, and German dive bombers attacked day and night. It seemed miraculous that any British soldiers, or their spur-of-the-moment pilots, would survive the German attacks and reach the shores of England. But after nine days, more than 300,000 soldiers were brought back to England. Equipment had to be left behind.

The Dunkirk "disaster" was a tremendous boost to England, a great moral victory. In *Their Finest Hour,* Churchill wrote: "In the midst of our defeat glory came to the island people, united and unconquerable; and the tale of the Dunkirk beaches will shine in whatever records are preserved of our affairs."

Before another month was over, France fell, and the sweep of the German army now seemed irresistible. The Wehrmacht broke through the famed Maginot Line as if it were made of tissue paper. Hitler's army reached Paris, and France signed a treaty with Germany at Compiègne,

also the site of Germany's capitulation in World War I.
Britain now stood alone.

Churchill knew that the British Isles were threatened
as they had never been before. In a stirring address, he
rallied his people to defense of the islands. Britain was
determined, he said, to fight to the last man. He ended his
speech saying, "If the British Empire and its Commonwealth last for a thousand years, men will still say, This
is their finest hour."

The Battle of France was over. The Battle of Britain
had begun.

Churchill drove himself, his Cabinet, and the war production chiefs to ends that seemed impossible to achieve.
He rallied the English people and instilled in them the
same confidence that he felt. Guns, ammunition, and
planes were produced at a feverish pace. Defenses were
increased. A home guard was established.

Hitler massed an invasion force on the French coast of
the English Channel. He screamed to the world that England would be wiped out, as quickly and with the same
ease that had forced France out of the war.

Hitler struck England from the air. In midsummer,
1940, the Luftwaffe swarmed over Britain, its heavy bombers dropping deadly explosives on ports, airfields, and industrial centers. Suddenly, London became the target for
the Luftwaffe and thousands of tons of bombs rained down
on the city. Hitler believed that if he could knock out the
capital of the British Empire, England would beg for
peace.

But the Nazi dictator underestimated the determination of the British people and their leader. Months went

by. England, although suffering greatly, showed no signs
of giving up the uneven battle. Instead, her air force, with
young British pilots in Spitfires and Hurricanes—fast,
maneuverable pursuit planes—stung like hornets at the
German bombers. Hundreds of German planes were shot
out of the skies.

Germany switched its *blitz* (lightning strike) from day
to night, and for two months, London was in flames almost every night. There could be little sleep as the noise
of exploding bombs, the roars of antiaircraft, and the
screams of sirens shook the city. Londoners by the thousands slept in shelters and in the tubes (the subway). In
the mornings, weary and red-eyed, they crawled out of
their holes and returned to their jobs, determined that no
Nazi foot would ever step on English soil.

German bombers spared few British cities, large or
small. Coventry, a city of nearly 300,000, was destroyed.

Churchill's stooped but stalwart figure was a familiar
sight to Londoners during those trying times. Air raids
did not deter his movements about the city. With a cigar
jutting from his grim mouth, wearing his siren suit, a
pale-blue, zip-up coverall, he would show up in air raid
shelters and take his place among shopkeepers and government clerks. By his very presence he would hearten
his fellow citizens as the thud of bombs shook the shelters
and brought destruction to the city.

After a blitz, Churchill would visit a devastated area of
London, mount the rubble, force his way through the
wreckage, and inspect the damage. People followed him
in droves. They wanted to touch him, to stroke his hand.
On one occasion, Churchill wept openly as he viewed

the devastation. At the sight of the Prime Minister crying, an old woman was heard to say, "You see, he really cares. He's crying."

To British people everywhere he had become their "Winnie."

14

◆◆◆◆◆◆◆◆◆◆◆◆◆◆◆◆◆◆◆◆◆◆◆◆◆◆◆◆◆◆◆◆◆◆◆◆◆

AMERICA ENTERS THE WAR

The German Luftwaffe kept pounding away at England, but it could not break British courage or morale. And that was Hitler's first real defeat. Churchill paid his respects to the magnificence of the Royal Air Force when he said: "Never in the field of human conflict was so much owed by so many to so few."

Britain received a measure of relief from the aerial bombardment in June, 1941. Violating his nonaggression pact with Russia, Hitler suddenly turned on the Soviets, his armies making a lightning strike toward Moscow.

To carry out the doublecross, a tactic for which Hitler became infamous, he had to pull some of his planes away from the British skies.

In a broadcast shortly after Germany's invasion of Russia, Churchill referred to Hitler as "this bloodthirsty guttersnipe." For years, Churchill had been openly anti-Communist. But now he assured Russia that Britain would give all the assistance she could. "The Russian danger," he said, "is ours."

Since the outbreak of the war, there had been a constant

exchange of correspondence between Churchill and Franklin D. Roosevelt, President of the United States. Roosevelt's admiration for Churchill increased as he saw the British leader rally the English people in the period of their greatest danger, and inspire them to magnificent efforts.

The Congress of the United States, due mainly to Roosevelt's urging, passed the Lend-Lease Bill on March 11, 1941. The United States could now supply Britain with American guns, tanks, aircraft, and ships.

Churchill and Roosevelt conferred on August 9–12, 1941, off the coast of Newfoundland. Both men took a great chance. Ships transporting the two leaders had to run the risk of being torpedoed by German submarines.

The men took an instant liking to one another. Their mutual trust and friendship carried on through the war years, and their teamwork played an important part in the Allies' final victory.

At the Newfoundland meeting, the two leaders discussed the peace aims of their respective nations, and the Atlantic Charter was drawn up. The charter, which was not publicly announced until August 14, contained eight points. It said, among other things, that Great Britain and the United States would respect the rights of all people to choose their own government. Churchill wrote: "The Atlantic Charter is not a law, but a star."

At the conference, Roosevelt asked Inspector Walter H. Thompson of Scotland Yard, Churchill's personal bodyguard during the war, how the Prime Minister was standing up under the stress and strain of his many duties. Thompson gave Roosevelt a favorable report. In his book

Assignment: Churchill, Thompson quotes Roosevelt as to
his feelings about Churchill: "Well, take care of him.
He's about the greatest man in the world. In fact, he may
very well *be* the greatest. You have a terrible responsibility
in safeguarding him. You have the responsibility of four
or five hundred million people."

It was only four months after the Newfoundland meeting that the Japanese—on December 7, 1941—attacked
Pearl Harbor. The sneak attack by Japanese aircraft
nearly wiped out America's fleet in the Pacific. President
Roosevelt asked the Congress to declare that a state of war
existed against Japan. On December 8, the United States
and Great Britain declared war on Japan, which, in turn,
declared war on those two nations. Germany and Italy
declared war on the United States three days later.
America had joined World War II.

Hopes rose for an Allied victory. Once again, as in
World War I, the United States had entered the conflict,
and a quick end to the war was envisioned. Only eighteen
months had elapsed between America's entry into World
War I and the end of the fighting. But this was not to be
the case in World War II. Four long years would pass
before VE Day—Victory in Europe—could be wildly
celebrated. Then more bloody weeks were to go by before
the atom bomb was dropped and Japan surrendered.

Hopes for a quick victory soon received a shocking set-
back. The Japanese, having knocked out America's Pacific
fleet, turned the fury of their air attack on two of Britain's
most powerful battleships plying the waters of the South
China Sea. The *Prince of Wales* and the *Repulse* were

sent to the bottom, severely crippling Britain's defenses in the Far East.

Great Britain was shocked by the loss of these mighty ships, and its rule of the seas was challenged. The Japanese moved swiftly, and in a short time they had captured Malaya, Burma, and Singapore.

After the loss of Singapore, the House of Commons attempted to censure Churchill's conduct of the war. It was the only such attempt during the entire battle, and it failed, largely due to Churchill's speech in the House: "I have never made any predictions except things like saying Singapore would hold out. What a fool and knave I should have been to say it would fall!"

The outlook was dark, indeed. In Africa, the tide was running strongly against the British. German and Italian soldiers, commanded by General Erwin Rommel, the "Desert Fox," were driving the British army across the Libyan desert toward the Egyptian border.

The United States was working around the clock to shift from peace to war production. As tanks, airplanes, and guns moved off the production lines, they were immediately shipped to England under heavy convoy. Men were being drafted into the American Army at a furious rate, but it took time to train and equip them. Ships had to be built for transporting American men and equipment to Europe, North Africa, and the Pacific. Britain and Russia pressed their appeals to the United States for supplies.

Churchill, carefully surveying the situation, decided that he must go to the United States. His fear was that

America would focus its efforts on the war in the Pacific. Churchill's belief was that the enemy, now fighting the Allies from two sides of the world, would first have to be defeated in Europe before it could be destroyed in the Far East. Churchill felt that by his presence in the United States, he could emphasize the necessity for keeping America's attention directed toward the European theater of war.

The Prime Minister was successful in his mission. He arrived in the United States about two weeks after the Japanese bombing of Pearl Harbor and America's entry into the war. He captured the hearts of Americans just as he had done with his own people.

On Christmas Eve, 1941, Churchill spoke from the White House balcony to a large gathering: "I spend this anniversary and festival far from my own country, far from my family, yet I cannot truthfully say that I feel far from home. Whether it be the ties of blood on my mother's side, or the friendships I have developed here over many years of active life, or the commanding sentiment or comradeship in the common cause of great peoples who speak the same language, kneel at the same altars, and, to a very large extent, pursue the same ideals, I cannot feel myself a stranger here in the centre and at the summit of the United States. I feel a sense of unity and fraternal association which, added to the kindliness of your welcome, convinces me that I have a right to sit at your fireside and share your Christmas joys."

Churchill's reference to his American mother further endeared him to the American public. He stressed his personal ties with the United States. In *The Grand Alli-*

ance, the third volume of his history of World War II, Churchill writes of his feelings in preparing his speech to a joint session of the United States Congress. The speech was delivered the day after Christmas.

"It was with heart-stirrings that I fulfilled the invitation to address the Congress of the United States. The occasion was important for what I was sure was the all-conquering alliance of the English-speaking peoples. I had never addressed a foreign Parliament before. Yet to me, who could trace unbroken male descent on my mother's side through five generations from a lieutenant who served in General Washington's army, it was possible to feel a blood-right to speak to the representatives of the great Republic in our common cause. It certainly was odd that it should all work out this way; and once again I had the feeling, for mentioning which I may be pardoned, of being used, however unworthy, in some appointed plan."

Churchill made four trips to Washington during the war, and he and Roosevelt met a total of ten times. An often-told anecdote refers to one of Churchill's visits to the White House. Roosevelt is said to have entered Churchill's suite at the White House just as the Prime Minister—stark naked—came out of the bath. Churchill welcomed Roosevelt with the words, "The Prime Minister of Great Britain has nothing to hide from the President of the United States." Questioned about the story later, Churchill disputed it by saying that he never received the President without at least a towel "around my middle."

Many months passed before there was any sign that the tide of war was turning. During this period, Churchill continued to be the inspiration of not only the British

people but of the entire world. At the age of sixty-seven
he worked an eighteen-hour day. His doctors worried
about him, but he refused to slow down. Churchill took
every opportunity to appear before the British people,
always with right arm outthrust, first and second fingers
spread in his "V for Victory" symbol. He also maintained
firm direction of Britain's effort in the arenas of fighting.
He advised his military leaders, but listened with considered care to their replies. He no longer overrode everyone as he had done as First Lord of the Admiralty.
Suggestions poured from him in an endless stream of
memoranda numbering over a million words. He formed
a small War Cabinet, patterning it after the one he had
served on in World War I. All reports from the field
came to the War Cabinet, bypassing many Cabinet Ministers who would normally receive these reports. Decisions
were reached quickly and made operational immediately.
Churchill was not only a great inspirational figure; he
was the man who held Great Britain's destiny in his hands.
And he never doubted that under his direction England
would triumph.

15

●●●●●●●●●●●●●●●●●●●●●●●●●●●●

TRIUMPH AND DEFEAT

The tide began to turn in the Allies' direction late in 1942. English General Bernard Montgomery hurled his Eighth army against Rommel at El Alamein in North Africa. The resulting battle was Britain's first decisive victory. Churchill said of it: "Before Alamein we never had a victory. After Alamein we never had a defeat."

A month later, the United States launched Operation Torch, and thousands of American troops poured onto the North African coast. The combined British and American forces struck at the Germans, and now it was the Desert Fox who had to retreat across the African sands. German resistance ended at Tunis, and the Allies now held the North African shores. Germany was driven from the continent by May 13, 1943.

Churchill, Roosevelt, and Stalin met three times during the war, at Casablanca, Teheran, and Yalta. At the Teheran conference, Churchill celebrated his sixty-ninth birthday. Typical was the way he insisted on being in charge of the affair. "I insist," he told the other two leaders, "that I be host at dinner tomorrow evening. I think I have one or two claims to preference. To begin with, I come first in seniority and alphabetically. In the second place, I represent the longest established of the three governments. And, in the third place, tomorrow happens to be my birthday."

Perhaps the most dominant of the three leaders, Churchill was always quite open in regard to the unstable tenure of his position as Prime Minister. In *Closing the Ring,* the fifth volume of his history, *The Second World War,* he wrote: "It was with some pride that I reminded my two great comrades [Roosevelt and Stalin] that I was the only one of our trinity who could at any moment be dismissed from power by the vote of a House of Commons freely elected on universal franchise, or could be controlled from day to day by the opinion of a War Cabinet representing all parties in the State. The President's term of office was fixed, and his powers not only as President but as Commander-in-Chief were almost absolute under the American Constitution. Stalin appeared to be, and at this moment certainly was, all-powerful in Russia. They could order; I had to convince and persuade. I was glad that this should be so. The process was laborious, but I have no reason to complain of the way it worked."

Churchill's opinion of Stalin again showed his prophetic nature. Although there was always tension between the two men, they could come to agreement on strategy. What repelled Churchill were Stalin's views on how German army officers should be treated when the war ended. The Russian leader flatly declared that thousands of them should be lined up and shot. Revolted by this statement, Churchill walked out of one meeting with the Russian dictator. Churchill also believed that Roosevelt was too soft toward Stalin, particularly concerning how Stalin and Russia would act when the war was over. Roosevelt believed that Stalin would be a reasonable man, that he could be dealt with at the peace table, and that Russia would not make any unusual demands. Churchill disagreed, and he was correct. Russian postwar demands resulted in a divided Germany, and later the erection of the Berlin wall. In addition, many central European nations became satellites of Russia.

On one broadcast, Churchill described the Soviet nation in these epigramatic words: "Russia is a riddle wrapped in a mystery inside an enigma."

The Big Three meetings were primarily devoted to discussing strategy, what next move the Allies would take against the enemy. Stalin wanted a second front opened in France at once. Churchill and Roosevelt finally convinced the Russian dictator of the absolute impracticability of such an operation at the present stage of the war. The Allies had just taken over control of North Africa. Stalin wanted the second front to relieve pressure on the Russian front, where German armies were still victorious.

Churchill provided the clinching argument against launching an invasion of France in 1942. He insisted that "rivers of blood" would flow into the English Channel. He wanted to strike at the Balkans—Yugoslavia, Romania, Bulgaria, Albania, Greece, and the European part of Turkey. Churchill described the Balkan peninsula as the "soft underbelly of Europe." He was, perhaps, harkening back twenty-five years when he had advocated the disastrous Gallipoli campaign which brought about his downfall.

Stalin and Roosevelt overruled Churchill on the Balkan proposal. A compromise was reached by the decision to invade Italy, striking first at Sicily, then moving on to the mainland. This did not please Churchill, for he wanted to strike directly at Rome. Calling attention to the Italian boot, he asked, "Why crawl up the leg like a harvest bug, from the ankle upwards? Let us rather strike at the knee!"

Again, Churchill was overruled. Sicily was invaded and captured, and Allied forces then invaded the mainland. Mussolini, the Italian dictator, was forced out of power and later hanged by his own people. Churchill commented on Mussolini in a broadcast: "The hyena in his nature broke all bounds of decency and even common sense." American and British troops moved up the Italian peninsula against savage resistance from the Nazis. Not until 1945 were the last remnants of Hitler's forces driven from Italy.

D day, the date for the invasion of France, was set at June 6, 1944. For days before, Churchill had insisted that he would go with the invaders, cross the English Channel, and be one of the first to set foot on the shores of France. General Dwight D. Eisenhower, Supreme Commander of the Allied Expeditionary Forces, absolutely refused to countenance such a foolhardy adventure. Churchill was a great leader. If he were killed in the invasion, the Allies would suffer an irreparable loss. At this time, Churchill was seventy years old. Despite Eisenhower's protests, Churchill was insistent. He was prevented from undertaking the risk only when King George VI said that if Churchill went, then the King would go, too. That finally convinced Churchill to abandon his idea.

On May 7, 1945, less than a year after the invasion of Normandy, Germany surrendered to the Allies. The fighting had been bitter, and thousands upon thousands of lives were lost. But the Allies had triumphed.

By one of the strangest twists of political fate, the Allies' triumph was Churchill's defeat. Less than three months after VE Day—Victory in Europe—Churchill had been voted out of office.

16

◆◆◆◆◆◆◆◆◆◆◆◆◆◆◆◆◆◆◆◆◆◆◆◆◆◆◆◆◆◆

<u>SIR</u> WINSTON CHURCHILL

Winston Churchill was deeply hurt by his political defeat, and for several days he maintained a brooding silence. Why had the British people rejected him only a few weeks after he had led his nation to victory in her most trying hour? For one thing, the English were tired, sick of war or anything relating to it. Churchill's Conservative party had been the war Government. The British people did not want a "war" Government to continue in peacetime.

Britain had also undergone years of rationing and lean times. Food, clothing, and shelter were in short supply. Clement Atlee and the Labour Government promised an end to Britain's wartime misery when they took over the Government on July 26, 1945.

But even at seventy, Churchill was much too resilient to continue brooding or to go into retirement. In fact, he came out of his short period of silence with a typical quip. King George VI offered Churchill the Order of the Garter, the highest order of knighthood in the British Empire. Churchill turned it down with the remark: "Why should I accept the Order of the Garter from His Majesty when the people have just given me the order of the boot?"

Churchill was also sorely distressed that he would have no part in the war effort against Japan in the Pacific. Victory over Japan came on August 14, 1945. In the week preceding Japan's surrender, the United States had dropped the world's first atomic bombs on the cities of Hiroshima and Nagasaki.

For Churchill, a most disturbing result of his defeat was that he would have little or no part in shaping the future and the peace, not only for Great Britain but for the world. But he had already made a tremendous contribution. When Churchill visited the United States in December, 1941, he and President Roosevelt had drafted a document which was to become known as the Declaration of the United Nations. The document reexpressed and elaborated the ideas that the two leaders had discussed in framing the Atlantic Charter. In June, 1941, fifty nations signed the United Nations Charter. From the Atlantic Charter had sprung the noble idea of the United Nations, an organization intended to settle all future military, political, and diplomatic disputes among the signing nations.

Churchill's friends now urged him to retire from the political arena and devote full time to his monumental *The Second World War*. They pointed out that it would not be proper for the world's greatest living statesman, the man who had led his nation to victory, to return to the House of Commons. But Churchill was having no part of this suggestion. "I am a child of the House of Commons," he stated with great dignity and solemnity.

Although no longer a political leader, Churchill continued his deep interest in world affairs. He was particularly concerned about Russia and feared that the Western democracies were not being firm enough with the Soviet Union.

Churchill first publicly used the phrase—"Iron Curtain" (which he coined)—in an address at Fulton, Missouri, where he had gone to accept an honorary degree: "From Stettin on the Baltic to Trieste in the Adriatic, an Iron Curtain has descended across the Continent. Behind that line lie all the capitals of the ancient states of Central and Eastern Europe: Warsaw, Berlin, Prague, Vienna, Budapest, Belgrade, Bucharest and Sofia. All these famous cities and the populations around them lie in what I must call the Soviet sphere. What is needed is a settlement, and the longer this is delayed, the more difficult it will be, and the greater our danger will become. From what I have seen of our Russian friend and ally during the war, I am convinced that there is nothing for which they have less respect than weakness, especially military weakness."

Churchill was the subject of heavy criticism because of his Iron Curtain speech. It was thought that he was much too hard on Russia. But time was to prove that once again he was correct.

Work on *The Second World War* was shared with his first love, the House of Commons. The writing of this history was a gigantic task, and Churchill was aided by a large staff of researchers who gathered and sorted material. As a history, *The Second World War* has been hailed by critics and historians as one of the greatest ever written. The six volumes were published between the years 1949 and 1954. It has been translated into many languages and is considered the standard reference work on World War II.

While writing his book and attending sessions of the House of Commons, Churchill was biding his time, planning another comeback. He wanted to be Prime Minister once more. He had a growing feeling that the British people would tire of the Labour party Government, and he was right again. In 1951, the Conservative party based its campaign on the high cost of living and on England's drop in prestige in Europe and the United States while under a Labour party Government.

The Conservatives won, and Winston Churchill was Prime Minister of Great Britain for a second time. During his following four years in office, prosperity came back to England, and her downward plunge toward being a second-rate power was checked.

Winston Churchill became Sir Winston in 1953. He had refused the Order of the Garter once, but he accepted it at the coronation of Queen Elizabeth II. A second great honor came to Sir Winston the same year. He was awarded the Nobel Prize for literature.

Churchill was eighty-one in 1955. He decided it was time to step aside for a younger man, and so he resigned as Prime Minister. This marked the end of Sir Winston's long, up-and-down political career, covering over half a century.

17

◆◆◆◆◆◆◆◆◆◆◆◆◆◆◆◆◆◆◆◆◆◆◆◆◆◆◆◆◆

"IN PEACE, GOODWILL"

Sir Winston Churchill had actively left the field of politics—national and international—which had so fully occupied his entire adult life. At first, his retirement must have been difficult. But he was the Renaissance man, the complete person. He occupied himself with his family, his dogs, his horses, his writing, his painting, and with the world around him.

Churchill spent his last years in his Chartwell Manor home and in a villa on the Riviera, surrounded by his family and a large entourage of secretaries. Although he was absent from any active participation on the international scene, the world still followed his daily life. A constant stream of reports on Sir Winston's activities was filed by newspaper, radio, and television correspondents. When he was ill—and he was ill several times—his condition became front-page news.

The great man went into retirement filled with honors. He had received medals and citations from nearly every nation in the world. In 1963, President John F. Kennedy, under authority of an act of the 88th Congress, proclaimed

Sir Winston Churchill an honorary citizen of the United States.

Sir Winston Leonard Spencer Churchill died on January 24, 1965. He was in his ninetieth year, and his death was not unexpected. He was an old man and he had been ill for a week. But even so, the world was shocked at the loss of this great statesman, this great war leader, this great human being. He had meant so much to so many.

Typical of Sir Winston, years before he had issued directions for his own funeral. He had stated that he wanted "lots of soldiers and bands." He had even selected the ten bands to be stationed at regular intervals along the route of the funeral procession. Admiring pomp and pageantry, he had specified the music of Beethoven and Chopin, to be played at the cadence of a measured sixty-five paces per minute.

The House of Commons assembled three days before the funeral while Sir Winston's body lay in state at Westminster Hall. There was but one vacant seat in the House —the one long occupied by Churchill. Prime Minister Harold Wilson bowed his head toward the vacant seat and said, "Where the fighting was the hottest, he was in it, sparing none, nor asking for quarter . . . [he] was a warrior, and a party debate was war. It mattered, and he brought to that war the conquering weapons of words fashioned for their purpose; to wound, never to kill; to influence, never to destroy."

The funeral cortege began its long, slow march from Westminster Hall, adjacent to Parliament where Sir Winston had served so many years. The procession moved up Whitehall, past the government houses, along the

Strand, and through Fleet Street to St. Paul's Cathedral.

Under gray skies and in bitter cold, a million men, women, and children stood with heads bowed in final respect. Millions more all over the world saw the procession on television via Telstar.

The gun carriage which bore the casket had first been used for the funeral of Queen Victoria in 1901. It was shrouded with the Union Jack, atop which lay a black velvet cushion bearing the diamond and gold regalia of the Order of the Garter.

St. Paul's Cathedral was packed with heads of state and with famous men and women from all over the world. In all, one hundred and thirteen nations were invited to send representatives to the funeral. One hundred and eleven did so. Only Communist China rejected the invitation, and the ambassador of Mongolia was too ill to attend. Dwight D. Eisenhower attended, as did Charles de Gaulle, Queen Juliana of The Netherlands, and the kings of Norway, Denmark, and Greece. Altogether there were gathered under the beautiful, lofty dome of St. Paul's Cathedral, four kings, two queens, five presidents, sixteen prime ministers, seven princes, and a grand duke.

The most notable honor to Sir Winston's memory was paid him by Queen Elizabeth II, the sixth monarch he had served. By attending the funeral, she shattered a British tradition. Never before had a British monarch attended the funeral of a commoner. But the Queen went even further. She arrived at the cathedral before Sir Winston's body was carried in. It is normal procedure for a reigning monarch to be the last to arrive at any state function and the first to leave. Before the eyes of the world Queen

Elizabeth II majestically paid Churchill her own personal tribute.

The funeral services lasted only thirty minutes. The service was preceded by the singing of the old "Church of England Hymn," written by John Bunyan, author of *Pilgrim's Progress:*

> "Who would true valour see,
> Let him come hither;
> One here will constant be,
> Come wind, come weather."

Churchill's favorite American anthem, "The Battle Hymn of the Republic," was also sung. He had requested it in issuing directions for his funeral. It was in honor of his American mother—and he had always thought it a stirring anthem.

As the service closed, voices were raised in the song "God Save the Queen." Then, dramatically, from the Whispering Gallery high in the dome of St. Paul's, there came the plaintive notes of "The Last Post," followed by the bugle call "Reveille."

When the services were ended, the body was carried from the cathedral and placed on the caisson, and the procession moved slowly through the streets to the Tower of London. There the casket was piped aboard the yacht *Havengore* and carried upstream on the river Thames to Festival Hall Pier. As the *Havengore* proceeded slowly up the river, a squadron of sixteen Royal Air Force jet fighter-planes swooped down low over the river, paying their respects to the man who had so honored them as the "so few" to whom so many owed so much.

From Festival Hall Pier, the casket was transported to Waterloo Station. The public ceremonies were over. Only the family and nearest friends accompanied the body on the seventy-mile train trip to Bladon where Sir Winston was interred in St. Martin's Cemetery, in view of Blenheim Castle, where he had been born ninety historic years before.

Eulogies were paid to Sir Winston by many notable statesmen. Among them was that of the late Adlai Stevenson, then United States Ambassador to the United Nations. He said: "Like the grandeur and power of masterpieces of art and music, Churchill's life uplifts our hearts and fills us with fresh revelation of the scale and reach of human achievement. Our world is thus the poorer, our political dialogue diminished and the sources of public inspiration run more thinly for us all. There is a lonesome place against the sky."

Years before, Sir Winston himself had written a brilliant summation of his unshakeable creed—and of his own life: "In war, Resolution. In defeat, Defiance. In victory, Magnanimity. In Peace, Goodwill."

◆◆◆◆◆◆◆◆◆◆◆◆◆◆◆◆

CHRONOLOGY

1874   Winston Leonard Spencer Churchill born in Oxfordshire, England, November 30.

1888   Enters Harrow.

1894   Enters Sandhurst Royal Military College.

1895   Churchill's father dies. Churchill receives Queen's Commission from Sandhurst. Travels to Cuba to view war between the island and Spain.

1896   Sails to India with 4th Hussars.

1897   Joins Malakand Field Force in battle against Pathan tribesmen. Writes first book, *The Story of the Malakand Field Force.*

1898   Joins 21st Lancers in battle against the dervishes. Writes *The River War.*

1899   Defeated in first stand for Parliament. Joins Boer War campaign. Is taken prisoner, escapes, and becomes national hero.

1900   Serves in South Africa.

1901   Wins seat in House of Commons as member of Conservative party.

1904   Joins Liberal party.

1908   Appointed president of the Board of Trade. Marries Clementine Hozier, September 12.

1910   Appointed Home Secretary.

1911   Becomes First Lord of the Admiralty.

1915   Resigns as First Lord. Rejoins army.

1916   Returns to House of Commons.

1917   Appointed Minister of Munitions.

1919   Appointed Secretary for War and Air.

1921   Appointed Secretary for Colonies.

1924   Named Chancellor of the Exchequer.

1939   Renamed First Lord of the Admiralty.

1940   Becomes Prime Minister, May 10.

1941   Meets with Roosevelt, August 9–12. Forms Atlantic Charter. Addresses United States Congress.

1945   Voted out of office as Prime Minister.

1951   Becomes Prime Minister.

1953   Receives Order of the Garter from Queen Elizabeth II. Awarded Nobel Prize for literature.

1955   Resigns as Prime Minister.

1963   Proclaimed an honorary citizen of the United States.

1965   Churchill dies, January 24.

INDEX